Letters to My Birthmother

ALSO BY AMY E. DEAN

Night Light
Once Upon a Time
Making Changes
Lifegoals

Letters to My Birthmother

An Adoptee's Diary of
Her Search for Her
Identity

Amy E. Dean

PHAROS BOOKS
A SCRIPPS HOWARD COMPANY
NEW YORK, NEW YORK

First published in 1991.

LIBRARY OF CONGRESS CATALOGING-IN-PUBLICATION DATA
Dean, Amy.
Letters to my birthmother :
an adoptee's diary of her search for
her identity / Amy E. Dean.
p.   cm.
ISBN 0-88687-615-X
1. Dean, Amy—Correspondence.   2. Adoptees—United States—
Correspondence.   3. Birthparents—United States—Identification.
4. Identity (Psychology)—United States.   I. Title.   II. Title:
Letters to my birthmother.
HV874.82.D43A4   1991
362.82'98—dc20   · 90-19869
CIP

Printed in the United States of America
Jacket design by Douglas & Voss Group
Book design by Fritz Metsch

Pharos Books
A Scripps Howard Company
200 Park Avenue
New York, NY 10016

10 9 8 7 6 5 4 3 2 1

Dedication

This book is dedicated to those who are adopted.

. . . open this book, and you'll get my life,
my version, my memory of it all.
—PATRICIA HAMPL,
BOOK REVIEWER, WRITING
ABOUT BOOKS OF MEMOIRS.

Contents

Preface

When I was thirty-one years old, I initiated a search for my birthmother through the adoption agency that had been responsible for my life when I was only a few days old.

The search was relatively easy. In less than three months, I was talking on the telephone to my birthmother.

But what has not been easy is processing how I feel now that I've found her. I ask myself: Why did I initiate the search? What did I hope to find? What do I need from my birthmother? How do I feel about her? Does the future hold anything for us?

These letters are my attempt to come to terms with some of the confusing and conflicting emotions that have dominated my heart and mind since I found my birthmother. They express my thoughts and feelings about growing up adopted, as well as my sentiments regarding the "search for my roots."

These letters are unmailed correspondences to my birthmother from the daughter she put up for adoption.

This book has been written to fulfill four needs of adoptees.

First, the book identifies and validates some of the thoughts, feelings, and behaviors that may be experienced by those who have been adopted. The adopted population in this country has been recognized by a wide range of published materials and support organizations. However, their particular issues and specific needs have not been identified, addressed, or fully understood by adoptive parents, friends and intimate partners, teachers, members of the helping community, or even adoptees themselves. Adoption *does* have an impact on the adoptee, whether or not he or she joins a caring and healthy family and is treated as "their own." Adoptees *are* affected by the fact that they are adopted and, because of this, often think, feel, and behave in ways different from those who are not adopted.

This book recounts the thoughts, feelings, and behaviors I've experienced as an adoptee at various times in my life. Others who are adopted may relate to some, most, or all of these because they are often *reactions* to the issues that are key to being adopted:

• *loss*
of a birth family, of a birth identity, and of an origin

- *vulnerability*
  to later losses or disappointments in life and to the possibility of other rejections or abandonments
- *identity difficulties*
  as a result of various concerns: the conflict of the dual identity of being a birth child and an adopted child; not matching or being similar in appearance to members of the adoptive family; a low self-image from being "unwanted" or feeling like "damaged goods"; and the feeling of being viewed forever as a child, not an adult, by legal restrictions and agencies that protect the adopted child even if that "child" is an adult
- *powerlessness*
  in birth and adoption circumstances
- *the need to know*
  the psychological need to solve the mystery of the adoption; the medical need to retrieve information about the genetic aspects of illness, physical features, and life span; and the historical need to discover personal genealogy
- *unresolved grief*
  over the original loss of a natural parent
- *fear*
  of being loved and being unloved; of separation, rejection, and/or abandonment; and of not finding birthparents before they die

The following list represents the thoughts, feelings, and behaviors I have experienced, and sometimes *still experience*, in reaction to my adoption. I include this list to motivate readers who are adoptees to think about how their own adoption influences various areas of their lives and to help readers who aren't adoptees to better understand those who are. Adoptees may find that they relate to a few, many, or most of these statements. If you're adopted, I encourage you to think about your own particular thoughts, feelings, and behaviors as well.

*The Thoughts, Feelings, and Behaviors I Have because I'm Adopted**

- I sometimes feel that I'll never "grow up."
- I'm sensitive to secrets and unshared information.
- I feel different from other people in a way that makes me feel misunderstood.
- It's extremely important that people like me.
- I sometimes overreact to changes over which I have no control.
- I'm highly sensitive to the needs of others and want to please them.
- I often feel chaotic, confused, or turbulent in love and/or intimate relationships.

---

*People who grew up in families where a dysfunctional behavior such as alcoholism, drug dependency, chronic illness, or verbal and/or sexual abuse existed may find that they, too, relate to many of these statements. But when analyzing personal reactions to these statements, I believe the distinction between those who grew up in a dysfunctional home and those who are adopted is that, for adoptees, *the impact and frequency* of these thoughts, feelings, and behaviors is much more resounding. I am both a child from a dysfunctional home and an adoptee. To me, these statements capture my sentiments and actions more accurately as an adoptee than as a person with a dysfunctional past.

- I fear separation, rejection, and abandonment.
- I sometimes blame myself for circumstances that are out of my control.
- I feel great sadness over any loss.
- I often demand perfection of myself and others.
- I sometimes feel sad, angry, or frustrated for no apparent reason.
- I spend a great deal of time thinking about or trying to resolve the issues surrounding my adoption.

Second, this book has been written to help those who interact with and/or care about adoptees understand the profound influence adoption has had upon them. According to "The Baby Chase," the cover story for the October 9, 1989, issue of *Time*, "Adoptees represent 2% of the U.S. population, yet by some estimates they account for one-quarter of the patients in U.S. psychological treatment facilities."

Adoptees have not been given the proper acknowledgment or understanding of the full impact that an adopted background has upon them, either by members of the helping profession or by those who love them.

For those readers who are not adoptees, I hope that this book will help you gain greater insight into what it feels like to grow up adopted so that you can better understand the thoughts, feelings, and behaviors of adoptees you know.

Third, this book has been written to encourage adoptees and those who care about them to make contact with others from similar backgrounds to exchange information, share feelings, and offer emotional support to each other.

Each of us, no matter what our particular needs or background, may desire to come together with others from similar backgrounds. It may be as basic a need as to identify with others like ourselves so that we don't feel so alone or as complex a need as to have others who can help us through common difficulties that are a result of our similar situations.

I feel that it's especially important for adoptees, no matter what their ages, cultural backgrounds, or adoption circumstances, to make contact with others who are adopted. It's equally important for those who care about adoptees—birthparents, adoptive parents, foster parents, spouses or intimate partners, friends, adoption case workers, teachers, medical professionals, and therapists—to make contact with those who share the common thread of knowing, caring about, or loving someone who is adopted.

You may choose to explore the option of joining or starting a support group. The American Adoption Congress (Cherokee Station, P.O. Box 20137, New York, NY 10028-0051), a national umbrella group for adoption support, search, and education, has member adoption support groups in various locations across the country. They can provide information about support groups near you and/or help you to start a group in your area.

If you're adopted and don't wish to seek out the support of persons in a group setting, at the very least I encourage you to make contact with others who are adopted and to talk about your feelings with them.

Finally, this book has been written to honor one of the most basic rights of any adoptee: the right to know. I believe that it's every adoptee's right to choose to search for one or both birthparents in adulthood, whether that search turns out to be a positive and joyous experience or a painful and heartbreaking ordeal.

The reasons adoptees choose to search are as varied as the adoptees themselves. Adoptees who make the decision to search can come from warm, loving adoptive families as well as from cold, nonnurturing adoptive homes. Those who search can be famous as well as unknown. They can be parents themselves or single. They can be young and old, male and female, dark-skinned and light-skinned, and rich and poor.

But the one common, basic reason most adoptees choose to search is simple: because they are adopted and they want to find out why.

It's my firm belief that the decision to search is highly personal and is often reached after years of agonizing consideration; therefore, such a decision should never be hampered by frustrating legal restrictions or nonsupportive parental judgments.

Children should not be brought into this world with the purpose of cloaking them in secrecy for the rest of their lives. The adult adoptee should never be denied the opportunity to search for his or her roots.

Acknowledgments

To Bonnie Broe, for her therapeutic guidance on the issues surrounding adoption and for her sensitivity in helping me to confront and deal with the particular losses in my life.

To Jeanie Lindquist, a friend and an adoptee, for her understanding about adoption issues and about the need to search for birthparents.

To Deborah Eaton, a friend whose sensitivity and nurturing during the writing of this book gave me the strength and courage to be not only an adoptee but also a writer.

And to Bruce and Sonja Dean, who understood that I needed to write this book so that I could "put my past to rest."

Author's Note

Although this book is based on the story of my adoption and my search for my birthmother, I've been sensitive to protecting the privacy of others. All of the individuals involved in this story—my adoptive father, my mother Sonja, my foster parents, the case worker at the adoption agency who handled my search, and, of course, my birthmother—were told that I was writing this book, with the goal of having it published. They were given the opportunity to have their names changed and/or identifying information about them revised to protect their anonymity if they so desired.

The names of my birthmother, her daughter, her husband, and the town have been changed from the actual names, per personal request. All other names and identifying information are true.

Letters to My Birthmother

Introduction

YVONNE KAYE, PH.D.

Author of *The Child That Never Was:*
Grieving Your Past to Grow Into the Future

Whether a child is adopted, illegitimate, fostered, or comes from other dysfunctional beginnings, that child often experiences grief as a result of the loss of normal childhood circumstances. Each child, in a particular fashion, pursues, agonizes, and obsesses over the losses in his or her life.

Adopted children often grow up pondering many loss-based questions even when they are adopted by loving and supportive parents. These questions include:

"Why was I given away?"

"Was I so bad that my mother/father couldn't bear to be with me?"

"Who were the people who gave me away?"

"Am I like these people?"

For adopted children, the most natural relationship in the universe—that between parents and the child they created—is splintered. Adopted children often mourn this loss of growing up with natural parents, even though they may never understand what they missed by not being with a natural family. Yet it is this "not knowing" that can cause problems in their growth, self-esteem, and self-confidence. What they missed in not being able to experience a natural family connection can also create a certain uneasiness, emptiness, and insecurity that may stay with them throughout their lives until they seek some resolution of their feelings.

Those who are adopted will relate very strongly to Amy's own struggles, to her desire to know who and what she lost. Although she and other adoptees have often been led to believe that they should leave well enough alone, adoptees face the sometimes psychologically confusing dilemma of needing to complete the unfinished business of resolving their grief over the loss of a relationship with biological parents while needing, at the same time, to not "rock the boat"—to be satisfied with what they have, not to yearn for what they *do not have.*

Amy, as you will see, discovered some answers to her childhood questions in adulthood as she searched for and found her birthmother. It was vital that Amy asked these questions and equally vital that she sought answers, for grief that is not dealt with in some way will continue to be experienced until it is resolved.

In my book *The Child That Never Was*, I write about the grieving needs of adults who come from "different" (dysfunctional) backgrounds. Their grief began in their past, when they lost all hope of experiencing a happy, normal childhood. When these people reach adulthood with unresolved grief, they often hear insensitive and invalidating statements designed to keep their grief suppressed or denied. Such statements include:

"Look at how you turned out; what can it matter now how you feel?"

"It was such a long time ago."

"It couldn't have been *that bad*."

But, as I state in my book, the bottom line in any person's recovery from childhood grief *is confronting and dealing with what was lost*.

Amy experiences various levels of grieving over her lost natural background. Dr. Elisabeth Kubler-Ross began the movement to appreciate the power of grieving with her book *On Death and Dying*. Because I am a thanatologist who works largely in the area of sudden death, as well as a counselor who helps those who have lived through the losses experienced in a dysfunctional childhood, I have adjusted Dr. Ross's stages of griving to formulate my own. These are:

- denial and isolation ("It didn't really happen"; "I must be the only one who feels this way—there's probably something wrong with me.")
- rage ("I'm angry over what I lost.")

3

- abandonment and helplessness ("I'm alone"; "There's nothing I can do.")
- ambivalence ("I don't know how I feel"; "I'm confused.")
- sadness ("I feel so unhappy.")
- adjustment ("What can I do to work through this?")

The process of grieving involves working through *all* these levels. Yet no one can be pushed from one level to another, nor do these levels necessarily flow one to the other until adjustment is reached. Sometimes, even when one level has previously been experienced, memories can trigger responses to return to that level and experience those feelings once again.

As you read Amy's sometimes heartrending letters in this book, you will be able to identify each of these levels of grief. For Amy, as well as for any adopted person who is grieving over the loss of natural parents, it is essential to complete a journey through these stages in order to move closer to recovery from loss.

When people can grieve over a person, place, or thing lost to them in such a way, there is some finality. For adoptees who wish to complete the "unfinished business" of resolving their grief, this book can be a beginning. Adoptees no longer have to be satisfied with what they have; they have a right to discover what they did not have and to address their feelings about this.

Amy needed to write this book for this express purpose. Her work is not only therapeutic; it also offers solace and optimism to those who are adopted and to those who interact with adoptees on any level. Amy had the courage to open her soul to her readers. This book shows her vulnerability as well as her strengths. Amy has touched me with this book.

Before the Search

Children are like wet cement. Whatever falls on them makes an impression.
　　　　—HAIM GINOTT

... society should recognize that growing up as an adopted child has certain differences....
　　　　—DR. STEVEN NICKMAN,
head of the adoption and custody unit of
Massachusetts General Hospital's child psychiatry
department, Boston, Massachusetts

August 15, 1984

Dear Woman Who Is My Real Mother:

It's a hot summer's night, and it's late. I sit at my desk, wearing a tank top and shorts, sweating. My grip on the pen is slippery; the edge of my hand sticks to the page. It seems as if both are conspiring against me (and in your favor) to try to slow me down and delay my desire to finally put into words the decision I reached earlier today, possibly the biggest decision I'll ever make in my entire life.

Today I made the decision to try to find you. Thirty years ago, for reasons I don't know, another decision was made—to terminate our relationship as mother and daugh-

7

ter. But, thirty years later, I'm still your daughter and you're still my real mother. These identities have not changed, despite the fact that you gave me up for adoption and I became someone else's daughter.

Reaching this decision today to try to find you wasn't easy. In reality, I think I've vacillated about it for years: should I, shouldn't I, should I, shouldn't I? It's as if I've been plucking a multitude of petals from a giant daisy ever since I initially realized I was adopted, when I first learned that my history began with someone who was a mystery to me. Like any mystery that remains unsolved for a long period of time, it yearns for discovery. Your whereabouts, your appearance, and your reasons for giving me up have pried at my imagination for years and tempted me to find the answers. But every time I thought I'd like to find you, I'd tell myself, "I shouldn't"—

I shouldn't because it might create problems—for you, for me, and for my adoptive parents.

I shouldn't because you might not want to see me.

I shouldn't because it's not what I'm supposed to do (adoption files are usually very difficult to open).

I shouldn't because it might show my adoptive parents that I don't love them.

I shouldn't because what's past should be kept in the past.

I shouldn't because "good" adoptees don't search.

I shouldn't because why would a thirty-year-old woman who already has a mother need another mother?

I shouldn't because it might be hard to handle the information I uncover.

But today I said, "I should," and all those shouldn'ts didn't seem to matter. Suddenly it became far more important to forge ahead in a search for you than to stay trapped in a web of confusion and mystery: a web that has been spun around me and my life; a web that has held me back from seeking answers to questions about who I was and where I came from. Where was I born? What time was I born? Was it a difficult birth? Did you see me? Hold me? Feed me? What did I do? How did you feel if/when you saw me? Did you smile at me? Did you see yourself in me? Who was my father? Did you love him? Why did you decide to place me for adoption? Was it hard for you to make that decision?

You're the only one who can tell me about my origins, my roots, my background—my "being born" story. To find you means I might learn the answers to all my questions. For this reason alone, I can justify a decision to search for you.

But, surprisingly, it was a bumper sticker I saw today that finally gave me the push to untangle myself from the web of mystery and confusion created by being adopted and to search for you. The bumper sticker read: ADOPTEES HAVE ROOTS AND RIGHTS, TOO.

As I drove behind that car for several miles, I thought about the meaning of that simple declaration. To me it meant that people who are adopted have origins or roots just like birth children, and they have the right to find their origins if they so choose.

You made a decision, thirty years ago, to release me from your life. It was your right to make that decision.

Today I made a decision that will go against your decision because it might possibly bring me back into your life. Because of this, there are those who may think that I shouldn't try to find you, that I should respect your right to remove me from your life. But I have the right to make a decision, too. You are my roots. You have my past. Now I want to claim it as my past, too. I can only do so by finding you.

My decision to search for you is my right. If or when I find you, you have the right to decide whether you want to see me.

But it's important for me to know that *I* am an adoptee who has roots and rights, too. It's very freeing to finally realize that I don't have to live my life as a character in a mystery if I don't want to. I can try to solve the mystery.

You are my mystery; *you* are my history. I need to find you.

August 16, 1984

Dear Nameless Person:

It's 3 A.M. and I can't sleep. I toss and turn, but I'm unable to relax. I want to know your full name. I can't seem to let go of this desire because your name was once part of my name—once part of my identity, once part of who I was.

I think people's names reveal much about who they are,

don't you? People's names often "fit" them. I think about my friends and try to imagine each of them with a different name. But different names seem to give them different identities. Wasn't it Shakespeare who wrote, "What's in a name?" To me, what's in a name is symbolic of the qualities and personality of the person it's identifying.

I remember one of my college professors who always used to call me by my first and last names. "Hello, Amy Dean," he would greet me when he saw me on campus. One day he explained why: "You know, your names seem to fit together very well. Amy Dean. I can't imagine just calling you Amy. It's got to be Amy Dean." I have another friend who, ever since we saw the movie *Come Back to the Five and Dime, Jimmy Dean, Jimmy Dean*, has called me "Amy Dean, Amy Dean."

My name is Amy Dean. Amy Elizabeth Dean. That's the name my adoptive mother and father gave me. This name is my identity; it fits me.

But my adoptive father once told me that my *real* name—the one you gave me—was Linda. Is that true?

I try to picture myself now as a Linda. It doesn't fit me as well as Amy does. When I look in the mirror, I see Amy and say "Hello, Amy." The name is safe, comfortable, and familiar; saying it makes me smile. When I look in the mirror and say "Hello, Linda," I frown and shake my head. It's amazing, the significance a name can have for a person's identity. I'm *your* Linda; I'm my adoptive parents' Amy. But who am I to *me?* (Sometimes I think my name identification could be written like a race horse's lineage: Amy out of Linda out of Birthmother.)

I wonder, if this story about my name is true, why you even gave me a name, an identification, before you let me go. Did it make it easier for you to say good-bye to a Linda rather than to an unnamed baby, to a Jane Doe?

As the years have separated us, did you ever wonder about your Linda growing up: where she was, what she looked like, what she was doing, how she was getting along?

I'm Linda. I'm Amy. I have two names.

But which one am I?

And who are you?

Later, August 16

Dear Person with My Past:

Questions, questions, questions! It's an hour later, and I still can't sleep. Now I want to know your nationality— my nationality, "our" nationality. I once asked my adoptive father, many years ago, "What's my nationality?" He responded by saying I was Scotch (because of the plaid skirt I was wearing at the time, he explained with a smile) and Italian (because I loved spaghetti, he chuckled). He thought he was being funny.

"Seriously, Dad, I want to know," I had replied. Perhaps it was the earnest look on my face that made his smile quickly fade. Or perhaps it was his realization that at some point in my life—and perhaps this was that point—I was going to start asking questions about the adoption and about my past.

He had shrugged his shoulders. "As far as I know, that's what you are. They didn't really tell us much when we adopted you. But I think I remember something about your being Scotch and Italian."

"But you don't know for sure? Couldn't I be something else?"

He had thought for a moment. "Well, I don't think so. They told us you were a good match for us. And I'm pretty sure they said you were Scotch and Italian."

"Am I Scotch on my mother's side or on my father's side?"

"Geez, Ame, I don't know. They didn't tell us anything about your mother or father. They just made sure you were a good match for us and that you were placed in a good home."

So I grew up a presumed Scotch and Italian girl, who was once Linda but who now was Amy, who was also "a good match."

A good match?!?

I can't help but feel angry now, thinking as an adult, at being labeled, as a child, with the phrase "a good match." I don't know how old I was when my dad and I had our "nationality talk"; I couldn't have been older than ten. Maybe I was even younger. But what must my child's ears have heard in that label, that I was "a good match?" To a child, "good" is an incredibly powerful word. When a child is good, positive rewards are often given: praise, hugs, kisses, extra treats, love, acceptance, nurturing. But when a child is the opposite of good—the dreaded "bad" —negative responses often follow: punishment, withholding love and affection, rejection.

What relief I might have felt at the time, knowing that I was "good." How lucky I might have believed myself to be, because if I hadn't been a good match (which had nothing to do with *who* I was as a person, but rather with how I "fit in" with my adoptive parents), then I could have been taken away from my adoptive mother and father. And maybe there wouldn't have been anyone who would have considered me a good match.

Can you imagine being called "a good match"? How would it make you feel? I'll tell you how it made me feel—like I was a *thing*, not a person.

Indeed, what *is* a good match? My understanding is that a good match is something or someone equal to or similar to something or someone else. In 1954, when I was adopted, I think I was termed "a good match" because I could "blend into" my adoptive parents' environment so effectively that no one would be able to tell that I wasn't their birth child. Such a good match meant that the circumstances of my birth could be kept secret and hidden. It meant that others wouldn't be tempted to ask questions, wouldn't try to uncover THE AWFUL TRUTH: that I didn't really belong, that I just "fit in," that I was a good match.

My being a good match dealt solely with appearances. It didn't even begin to scratch the surface of feelings and emotions that resulted from the reasons why I was given the label in the first place.

Dear Woman Who Gave Me Up:
Ever since I made the decision last week to search for you, I haven't been able to get one peaceful night of sleep. I toss and turn. I'm nervous and edgy. I've begun smoking again, even though I have asthma (do you have asthma, too?) and haven't smoked in over ten years. I'm confused about my decision to search for you: Am I doing the right thing? Or should I let things stay the way they are, with our lives separate? I attempt imaginary conversations with you: "Hi, uh, I'm your daughter. . . ." I ponder how I should address you if/when I find you: Mom, Mother, Ma, Mama, Mommy, Mrs.————, Ms.————? I examine my face in the mirror and wonder what parts of me match parts of you: Are our eyes the same? Our hair? The shape of the face? The nose?

And all this simply because I made a *decision* to find you! I haven't even begun the *process* of a search!

Yesterday, when I stared at my face in the mirror, I suddenly burst into tears. I cried for hours, sucking in great gulps of air while hot tears flowed down my face and plopped to the floor. It was as if all the emotions I had ever felt about being adopted had bubbled to the surface and spilled over—feelings of pain, sadness, rejection, abandonment, loneliness, guilt, shame, and low self-worth. Unless you're adopted, you can't imagine what it's like to be adopted or understand all the feelings you carry around with you because someone initially didn't want you, for whatever reasons. (Just as I can't imagine what it feels like for you to be a birthmother unless I, too, had given up my child at birth.)

I wonder now if I'm strong enough to follow through with my conviction that searching for you is not only my right but also my desire. My right to find you is based on an intellectual decision: You're my mother and I'm your daughter, and we both have a right to know who each other is. But the *desire* to find you has an emotional basis, one that's heartfelt, one that means I need to become vulnerable and open—to reexperiencing my feelings about being adopted; to remembering, once again, what my unhappy childhood was like; and to risk seeking you out, the person who initially rejected me and abandoned me and who might possibly reject me again.

My desire to find you goes deeper than finding out the answers to questions about who I was and where I came from. It's more than a need to know my name and nationality.

My desire to search for you is a way for me to resolve the confusing array of feelings I've felt as an adoptee. I've lived for years feeling like there was a shadow over me, feeling as if I've been out of step with the pace of the rest of the world, wondering if I could ever feel like I belonged anywhere. I've felt emotionally insecure and lacking in self-confidence. I've been restless and frustrated and often plagued by feelings of guilt and shame.

But will I be able not only to handle the emotional upheaval caused by remembering what it has felt like to grow up adopted, but also to allow you in my life if/when I find you?

I realize now that my search for you will also be a search for myself, a search for the child within me, who lives with the label of being adopted and has been able to enjoy the benefits, as well as the hardships, of having such a label.

August 21, 1984

Dear Creator of Me:

As I wrote in my last letter, there are opposing consequences to being adopted: benefits as well as hardships. Most people would consider it a benefit of adoption to be placed in a home with two loving parents. In my case, however, this was not a benefit. I can't explain why in this letter. As I've mentioned to you, so many emotions are crying out for my attention since I made my decision to find you that even writing these short letters drains me, wipes out my energy, saps my strength. I need a little more time; there are some memories I've buried so deeply that the thought of exhuming them feels threatening and scary.

But, I promise you, I will tell you about my adoptive

home soon. For now, in this letter, I'd like to tell you about some of the benefits and hardships I experienced as a result of being adopted.

In the years before I entered the fifth grade, I wore the label of "adopted child" proudly. So many children *dream* that they're adopted, and I really was! My friends envied me. It was great to be able to puff out my chest and declare: "I'm adopted. My parents *picked* me out from a whole bunch of babies. Your parents got *stuck* with you. Nah, nah. . . ."

Although I didn't have a "being born" story like other children (which included how they "behaved" in their mother's womb, what hospital they were born in, and at what time they were born), my adoptive father would tell me about the first time he laid eyes on me: "You were just a little baby. The minute I saw you, it was love at first sight." His sensitive, gray-green eyes would fill with tears of joy and happy memories. Then he'd smile at me—a smile that would light up my heart because I would know that it was just for me—and he'd say, in exactly the same way every time (but I never tired of hearing it): "You were so cute. You had a pink bunny suit on. I was so happy."

To me, my "being born" story was just as good as, if not better than, my friends' stories.

Indeed, my adoptive father always showed me, in his words as well as his actions, that I was his special little girl. I was never treated differently because I was adopted, although I was an only child and a little spoiled. My father and I rarely spoke about my being adopted. Indeed, I considered my dad to be my "real" father, and he raised me as his "real" daughter.

But as I grew older, the symbol of adoption I had once proudly worn began to be a stigma. Up to that time, I had thought about adoption as *selection*. I had been chosen, my dad had told me, and I saw that as great.

However, my peers soon taught me that the flip side of selection is *rejection*. The friends who had once envied me now turned on me with cruel comments:

"If you're picked out, it means you can be taken back if nobody likes you."

"My parents call me theirs because they really had me. Your parents didn't really have you."

"You don't look at all like your parents. I look just like mine. My eyes are blue like theirs. You don't look like anybody."

"You must've done something awfully bad for your real mother to give you away."

Instead of believing that adoption meant being chosen, I began to believe that adoption meant rejection, being "put up for grabs" because someone didn't want me. The older I became, the less special it seemed to be adopted—and the more questions I began to ask about who I was and why I was put up for adoption. I wanted to know where I came from, beyond the saga of the birds and the bees. I needed to understand *why* I was adopted and the circumstances of my adoption.

The biggest hardship I had to deal with, in growing up

as an adopted child, was knowing that I was adopted but not knowing why. Not knowing why made me look at myself critically and wonder what was so wrong with me that my own mother and father wouldn't keep me. Not knowing why kept me in the dark and made me sensitive to secrets or the whispered conversations of others (I always thought they were talking about some failing in me that had led to my adoption). Not knowing why took away part of my identity; I had to adapt, like a chameleon, to a new environment and to assume the background, personality, and character traits of a new family without knowing *who* I really was before I had to change.

When I asked my adoptive father why I was adopted, he told me that all he knew was that my "real" parents couldn't take care of me. But I wasn't satisfied with that explanation. I wanted *to know why.* I wanted to know why so I could *understand.*

My father could have lied to me about the circumstances of my adoption. He could have invented a logical reason— the death of my parents, an unfit mother, sickness, etc. —and he certainly wouldn't have been the first adoptive parent to do so. But he never did, and for that I'm grateful. He was honest with me, even though he must have known that this honesty was difficult and frustrating for me to hear. But he brought me up to never live in a lie and to always be truthful, even if the truth didn't always provide the answers.

Because my father couldn't help me, I took matters into my own hands. I tried to figure out the reasons for my adoption on my own.

My first theory about my adoption was that my real parents had died in a tragic automobile accident. I liked this scenario best because no one can argue with death. Fantasizing that my birthparents were dead meant that they had had no choice in my adoption. So I hadn't been rejected after all; my parents weren't around anymore to take care of me, and somebody had to. Case closed.

Another of my theories was that my birthparents were famous people—Hollywood actors, Pulitzer Prize-winning newspaper reporters, television producers, or renowned scientists—who traveled extensively and were too busy to take care of me. So they let me be adopted, with the stipulation that they would take me back when they had more time to spend with me. (I sometimes enjoyed this "on loan" adoption theory when I wasn't getting along with my parents. Then I would tell myself, "So what if I'm being punished now? Soon my *real* parents will come to take me home. And they'll let me do whatever I want! *They* won't punish me.")

Another theory focused less on my birthparents and the adoption and more on limitations I believed I had as an individual. Rather than think of myself as adopted, I surmised that I was my adoptive parents' real child but was suffering from a rare form of amnesia that prevented me from knowing a lot about my past. This theory was based on my observation that all the kids in school knew a great deal about themselves and their families. They seemed to be connected with who they were and where they came from in a very natural way.

Thus, I concluded, my problem was based on a matter

of time—when my memory would be restored—and not on a matter of genetics.

Once I had reached the diagnosis of *amnesia unknownus*, I wondered how long it would be before my memory came back. I felt it couldn't be soon enough; I wanted to escape from the many awkward situations that faced me because I lacked appropriate information about me that I needed to know.

One such awkward situation involved a fifth-grade school assignment. At the time, classroom teachers weren't as sensitive to the different home life situations of their students as they are today. The assignments they gave were geared to the majority of students who came from homes that had a "real" mother and a "real" father living under the same roof.

I'll never forget the homework assignment. It intensified the amnesia-like symptoms I believed I suffered from and validated how different I felt from other children.

The task was simple: to create my family tree. The teacher explained the assignment to the class: "I want you to go as far back as you can in time to record the members of your family on a family tree like the one I have diagrammed on the board. Begin with your parents and your aunts and uncles and cousins. Then record *their* parents and their aunts and uncles and cousins. Go even further back to record *their* parents and aunts and uncles and cousins. And so on. Some of you may even be able to trace your ancestors back to the time of the landing of the *Mayflower*. Just imagine that, children. I think you'll find this assignment fascinating!"

Ugh, I thought to myself. How fascinating could a blank piece of paper be? I didn't know how I'd do the assignment. I had no idea who *I* was, so how could I possibly know who *my* family was?

Embarrassment crept in. I pictured what would happen the next day, when the assignment was due, when I would be called on to stand up in front of the class with my homework. . . .

Slowly I arise from my desk and walk the interminably long walk to the front of the class. Then I turn to face the class. I look out over the sea of staring faces. My vision wavers; suddenly the familiar faces of my schoolmates look weird, even menacing. I look away and focus on a dust kitty on the floor. Then I mumble, "I couldn't do my assignment because I don't know my ancestors." The faces of my schoolmates register astonishment. Some turn around in their chairs and whisper to friends. The teacher's jaw drops at my pronouncement. She demands silence. As the room grows quiet, she slowly arises from her wooden swivel chair, its creaking and groaning joints seeming to complain directly to me. Then she folds her arms across her chest and peers down at me.

"And just why didn't you do this assignment, Amy?" her words slice into the air.

"Be-because I'm adopted and I don't know my real f-family!" I splutter in reply, then race back to the sanctuary of my seat.

The classroom explodes with gales of laughter. The children point at me and my face turns a bright, bright red because I have been voted the best blusher in the class and this is certainly a prime blushing situation.

And amid the roars of all the children—and the teacher, who

never ever laughs but who now finds my situation quite amusing—I
slouch low in my chair and glance nervously around me at the
elaborate and completed family trees on the other children's desks
and feel such intense jealousy for those who have what I
haven't—a foundation to their lives, a basis from which to work,
a connection, a meaning—knowledge.

But my fifth-grade assignment didn't turn out like my anxiety fantasy at all. I told my father about the project when he came home from work. After dinner, he helped me. He named *his* parents and grandparents and *his* sisters and brothers and their sons and daughters, and so on. He helped me to create the *Dean* family tree.

Even though I was legally a Dean and happy to be one, I wanted to cry out: "But that's not my *real* family! I need to know about *my* family! That's not *me*! I need to know about the family I came from!"

But I kept silent, because I was a Dean and no one, even my father, knew me as otherwise.

Another place where I felt the awkwardness and confusion about my unknown past was in doctors' offices. When I was younger, my parents filled out my medical forms. It wasn't until I was much older, when I was in high school and college, that I started filling out the forms myself. I had no problem providing information about childhood diseases—mumps, measles, and so on. I knew all about them; I had lived through them.

But I had no idea about my family's medical history.

Diabetes? Cancer? Heart conditions? On every doctor's form, I recorded my family's medical history as "I don't know."

To me, this was yet another hardship of being adopted: to reach adulthood with no more information about myself than I had when I was a child.

To have no knowledge about my adoption, to have no family heritage, and to have no medical history are the hardships I've had to endure in growing up adopted. In effect, I've grown up from an "adopted child" into an "adopted adult"; the age and the label have changed, but the need to know is still the same.

It's *you* who knows. In finding you, I hope to find me.

August 22, 1984

Dear Source of Information:
Why do *I* have to try to locate *you* to find out information about *me?*

Shouldn't *you* be required to contact *me?*

August 25, 1984

Dear Birthmother:
Do you realize that these letters are my first attempt to

put into *words* how it feels to be adopted? The only other time I came close to communicating how I felt about being adopted was with another adopted person I met years ago at summer camp. The conversations she and I had were fun and exciting—certainly not painful, as these letters are to write! But I do remember that our parting was painful. . . .

Do you remember what I wrote in an earlier letter, that no one, unless they're adopted, knows what it feels like to be adopted? It's true. I felt very lonely growing up, with no one who could relate to what I was feeling. But then, during the summer when I was fifteen years old, I met another adopted person at an overnight camp.

Her name was Amy, too. She had the same last initial as I did, **D**. She had short, straight brown hair and brown eyes, like me. She and I had the same build. We were the same height. We were the same age. And, once we discovered we were both adopted, we became inseparable.

We shared so many similarities with one another that we surmised we were sisters by birth who were drawn together, by a fluke of fate, to finally meet at the same summer camp. We spent most of that summer off by ourselves or lying together on a cabin bunk bed, talking ceaselessly, wondering what our real mother was like, why she had given us up for adoption, and why we hadn't been adopted into the same family. We pondered ways we could eventually live together and be reunited with our real mother and father, who would be overjoyed to find us again (we had become separated from them while shopping in a large department store) and who would take us back with open arms (they hadn't had any other children because they were so devastated over their loss of us). Our story would have a happy ending, just as all the stories we read at our age did.

Amy helped me feel as if I had a twin, a connection, a soul mate. She was someone who understood the loneliness I felt inside when I thought of myself as a "second-hand child." She and I shared a bond that I've since been unable to duplicate with another human being, a bond that came not only from the common circumstance of our being adopted, but also from our desire to belong together because of our similar appearance. (I've always been envious of "The Brady Bunch" family. Even though the six children had different sets of parents, all the girls "had hair of gold, like the mother, the youngest one in curls" and the boys all looked like their birthfather, Mike Brady, who had dark, curly hair and twinkling blue eyes.)

At the end of the summer, Amy and I desperately clung to each other and cried with heartfelt sadness because we knew that our dream of being together wouldn't come true.

My parents and Amy's parents eventually separated us tearful, clutching girls on the last night of camp, escorted us to our separate cars, and drove us to our homes, miles apart from one another.

Amy and I wrote to each other for a while, but our separate lives and the geographic distance between us prevented us from ever recapturing the connection we had felt that summer at camp.

I returned to camp the following summer, but Amy didn't. I never saw her again.

I realize now that Amy was more than a soul mate to me and more than a person who had a similar past. Amy was a confidante, someone with whom I could share the secret of my adoption and my innermost feelings about being adopted. Growing up adopted was difficult enough; having no one to talk to about it made me feel even more alone and misunderstood.

So I learned to keep my feelings to myself and my fantasizing in my own head, because no one else seemed to understand, as well as Amy did, what adoption was all about.

August 28, 1984

Dear Person Who Started Things Off:

To me, adoption centers on two powerful feelings: of being lost and of grieving about loss.

I feel lost because I don't have biological ties to a parent or parents or to a family. I feel lost because I don't know my "being born" story (I only know my "being adopted" story.) I feel lost because I don't know anything about my past. I feel lost because I don't know my medical history.

I simply feel lost.

I also feel like I'm constantly grieving about loss. You left me alone, without a real mother. You're the original loss in my life. I feel the impact of this loss any time I experience other losses in my life. If I lose a friend, it's not just the friend I lose; I lose the friend and you. If I lose a pet, it's not just the pet I lose, but the friend, the pet, and you. If I lose something, like a softball game, it's not just the game I lose, but the friend, the pet, the game, and you.

It's difficult for me to deal with losses as they occur, on an individual basis. They overwhelm me. I can't seem to keep them in perspective. Instead, the losses in my life seem to pile up, one on top of the other, until it seems that all I've had in my life, since Day One, are losses.

My life of loss begins with you. Can it end with you, too?

September 4, 1984

Dear You:
Do you know anything about loss? Do you feel like you've lost me? Or is it impossible to lose something you never really wanted to have?

September 8, 1984

Dear Uncaring Person:
I hate you!
It's all your fault!
It's 5 A.M. and I've just awakened from a horrible

dream. In this dream, I'm nine years old. I'm at school. It's recess time. I'm at the playground with all the other kids, waiting to be picked for one of the two playground kickball teams.

I line up with everyone else after the captains are appointed, then wait, eagerly listening for my name, almost holding my breath, because I don't want to miss the call. I start out very hopeful, very excited. I smile, stand tall, look each captain in the eye, and try to exude confidence. I want to scream, "Pick me! Pick me! I know I can kick the ball farther than anyone else, run faster around the bases, and catch any ball the other team kicks, even if it goes high in the air. *Please*—just try me. *Just give me a chance.*"

I wait. The kids who are chosen race from their places around me to their respective captains' lines. The line behind each captain grows longer; the line of remaining players shortens.

My smile fades. My shoulders slouch. I look down at the ground. I'm no longer confident. I want to say to myself, "Forget it, it's no big deal," and to believe it, but it *is* a big deal.

Instead I think, "If I was any good, I'd have been chosen by now. But I'm not. I stink. I'm no good. I don't deserve to even be on a team. *Nobody wants me.*"

This is all your fault! You've made me into a "second-hand child." You've made me feel as if nobody wants me.

What gives you the right to have me and then walk away? Were you glad, when you gave birth to me, that I was "a good match"? Did the adoption people tell you not to worry about me, that someone would eventually want me? Did you say "Great!" and then throw your clothes on and walk out into a new, sunny day, the first day of the rest of your new life without me?

I want you to answer this: What was so god-damned wrong with me that you gave me up? Tell me: Why did you even bring me into this world?

You made things turn out the way they did in my life.

It's all your fault.

September 9, 1984

Dear Birthmother:

I'm glad I got mad at you yesterday.

It seems that I've spent most of my life trying to please other people. I've never believed I've had the right to say "No," the right to refuse a request, or the right to show my anger. I've been afraid that people won't like me and will leave me if I don't give them what they want or need or if I don't act in ways they deem acceptable. I've struggled with this "people pleaser" element in my personality for most of my life; the underlying hope is that I'll find the right "formula"—the "right" way to think, feel, and act—that will guarantee that *no one* will ever leave me again.

So it's a step in the right direction when I can genuinely

express how I'm feeling, without editing or altering the impact of the emotion, because that means I'm willing to risk the possibility that I might not be liked or I might be left.

But I wonder: Am I able to be angry with you because you're not in my life, because you've already left me?

Will I be able to show you my anger if we ever meet? Will I be willing to risk losing you again?

September 15, 1984

Dear Decision Maker:

Have you ever regretted the decision you made to let me go? Have you ever thought, "I hope my little girl is doing okay?" Have you ever wondered about me, how I turned out, what I look like, what my adoptive family is like, what I've done with my life, and what I'd like to do in the future?

Have you ever cared about me?

Have you ever loved me?

September 20, 1984

Dear Woman Who Left Me:

I don't know why I asked you in my last letter if you loved me. What does it matter? You're not with me.

I don't know why I'm even searching for you. What does it matter? You didn't raise me or take care of me.

What does it matter?

Phil Collins sings a song in which he laments, over and over again, "I don't care anymore . . . I don't care anymore . . . I don't care anymore. . . ."

What does it matter?

I wish I could say, "I don't care anymore." I wish I could say, "Nothing matters to me."

But there are things that do matter to me—

Consistency.

Being there.

Not walking out.

Not going away forever.

Love that doesn't hurt or feel empty.

Being part of a family.

Do you know what happens when you cup your hands together and try to hold water in them? You can keep the water in your hands only if you squeeze your fingers tightly together and make sure your hands don't separate from one another. But once you grow tired, or you shift your position, or your nose begins to itch, slowly the water will drain out of your grasp.

The "waters" of my life—the people I needed and loved and the ideal family I've always wanted—have drained out of my life, even though I've desperately tried to hold them in my grasp.

I've lost you, I've lost my adoptive mother, and I've lost a family.

What does it matter?
Should I care anymore?

September 24, 1984

Dear First Mother:

From the moment I woke up this morning, I knew I'd write you tonight about the circumstances of my life after you let me go. I knew this because I've realized, in thinking about what I wrote in my last letter, that I *do care*, that things *do matter* to me. In fact, they've always mattered to me. I guess if I didn't care, if your role in my life didn't matter, then I wouldn't want to find you.

But I do.

It's just hard for me to look ahead, to wonder what might happen if/when I find you. I'm scared to risk your rejection or abandonment because I'm fragile at times, easily shattered. I think back to my past and wonder: "Could this happen to me again?"

But I guess that in order for me to look ahead, I need to look back and to try to let go. All day, I've thought about this letter. Now it's 7 P.M., the dinner dishes are done, and there are no more diversions to keep me from my task.

I'm ready to take you back to my childhood.

I'm ready to look back.

I wish I could begin by assuring you that I was adopted into a loving home, that I was brought up by a happy and

34

healthy adoptive mother and father, and that I've lived happily ever after.

But that wouldn't be the truth. Perhaps if it were the truth, I might not be searching for you now. I don't know. But I do know that the circumstances that occurred in my life after I was adopted weren't part of the normal, or even expected, chain of events. Despite the fact that I might have been "a good match" for the couple who adopted me, my adoptive mother wasn't a good match for me.

She was an alcoholic.

The adoption agency's case workers didn't know this when they interviewed Bruce and Margery Dean, a sober, capable, and loving couple who wanted to adopt a baby and give the child a happy home. My adoptive father didn't know this because he thought Margery drank to cope with her disappointment and depression over their inability to conceive children. My adoptive mother didn't know this because she was doing what she had done for ten years of their marriage—drinking every day while she fulfilled the role of the responsible, dedicated wife of a successful businessman.

Nobody knew this until *after* I was placed with the Deans on February 19, 1954. I was almost five months old, had been renamed Amy Elizabeth Dean, and was regarded by my adoptive parents as what they needed to make a healthy, happy, and whole family.

But we never became a healthy, happy, and whole family. Margery didn't stop drinking. Her drinking wasn't a well-kept secret. My adoptive father would leave for work in the morning and worry about me all day, wondering whether Margery was drinking and how she was taking care of me. Neighbors noticed her erratic behaviors caused by the drinking. They sometimes rescued me from the street outside my home, where I could be found wandering in my diapers. They became concerned when they witnessed her staggering out of the house, drunk, with me in her arms, and watched as she placed me in the car and drove off with me.

Because of Margery's drinking, I was temporarily taken away from my adoptive parents on May 14, 1956, and placed in a foster home. I was almost two and a half years old. "Mom" and "Dad" Fowler were the foster parents appointed by the adoption agency to take care of me while Margery tried to resolve her drinking problem.

Three months later, I returned to live with my adoptive parents. But one month later—to the day, in fact—I was placed once again under the care of Mom and Dad Fowler. I stayed with them until September 26, 1958. During those two years, my parents divorced and my adoptive father was granted custody of me. He spent every weekend with me until he hired a housekeeper to take care of me so that he could bring me home to live with him. Then he remarried on April 7, 1961.

Margery left me shortly before my third birthday.

I never saw her again.

By the time my adoptive father remarried, I was seven years old and had had four mothers: you, Margery, Mom Fowler, and my father's second wife, Sonja.

Shortly after Sonja came to live with my father and me,

I visited some of the neighbors and asked the women if they would be my mother. I believed that Sonja would leave me as Margery had, so I figured I needed to have other mothers lined up, ready to step in to take her place.

I *expected* another change to occur in my life, even though it never did.

Can you understand now my need to find you and to connect with you in some way? I don't want to feel abandoned or rejected for the rest of my life. I don't want any more losses.

Can you understand now my anger at you and why I might blame you, why I might say, "It's all your fault?" Sometimes it's hard to think about (or let alone *feel*) the losses I've had in my life. I grew up feeling helpless and powerless. I've had no choice, no voice, and no control over the circumstances that have involved me. You put me up for adoption. I couldn't control that. Margery was an alcoholic. I couldn't control that. I lost Margery as a full-time mother. I couldn't control that.

So I need a source where I can vent my anger and frustration.

Sometimes I think you've caused all these changes in my life to happen. I reason: If only you had held on to me, I never would have had to experience so much pain, so much loss.

Sometimes I blame Margery. I reason: If only she had recovered from her alcoholism, then my adoptive family would have been healthy, happy, and whole.

Sometimes I blame my father for not making everything right, although I can never identify what it is he could have done to make things better. He certainly couldn't have stopped Margery from drinking. I believe he did the best he could to make my life as normal as possible, given the circumstances.

But more often, I blame myself. I feel like I've failed as an individual. I think of myself as "damaged goods" and am extremely critical of myself. I believe that if only I had been better, smarter, thinner, quieter, prettier—whatever—then I never would've been left.

The effects of my childhood circumstances on who I am today can be likened to what happens when a rock is tossed into a placid lake. Where the rock explodes through the glassy surface of the lake, the water splashes up. Margery's drinking was the rock that was tossed into the hoped-for security of my adoptive family.

After the rock enters the water, ripples play over the entire surface of the lake, not just where the rock enters. Losing Margery as my adoptive mother affected various areas of my life for many years.

But I'm unlike the lake in one important way. The lake is fluid. It takes the disturbed waters only a short time before the ripples smooth out and the stillness on the water's surface is restored.

Even today, it's hard for me to calm down, to reach a certain stillness within. I feel great inner turmoil especially when I'm involved in an intimate relationship. I'm miserable when I need to be emotionally and physically close to someone. I cry a lot. If I'm told "I love you," I feel depressed and sad. I'm possessive and clingy. I doubt the love and tenderness that's shown to me. I apologize frequently for no real reason. I feel grateful that someone chooses to spend their valuable time with a worthless person such as myself. I don't trust natural separations that occur in relationships; instead, I believe that any time spent apart signals the end of the relationship. I live in constant fear and anxiety that I'll be left (again).

In searching for you, I'm seeking to establish some bond, some connection, some intimacy. This causes me great inner turmoil.

I wonder: If I find you, will you leave me again?

September 28, 1984

Dear Birthmother:
I think it's time for me to tell myself, "Enough already, Amy! Stop focusing on the losses in your life. *Find* things; don't keep hanging on to everything you've ever lost or believe you'll have the potential to lose, or you'll stay stuck in your pain, frustration, and confusion for a long, long time."

For how can I lose you when I haven't even found you?

October 3, 1984

Dear Woman Who Gave Birth to Me:
Thirty-one years ago today, you brought me into this

world. If someone had told you back then that your daughter would want to find you over three decades later, would you have believed it?

Well, believe it! I'm ready to take the risk and to try to find you. In fact, earlier today I took the next step. I called the Worcester Children's Friend Society, the agency that handled my adoption, and asked the woman who answered the phone how to go about trying to locate my birthmother. I thought she'd tell me that I couldn't search for you or that I'd have to hire detectives, get a lawyer, or go to court. Instead, she informed me that the agency is handling searches for its clients—both adoptees and birthmothers—who request them.

Imagine that!

That means that whenever I'm ready, the agency is ready to meet with me and help me begin my search.

What a birthday gift—just waiting for me, when I'm ready to open it.

October 11, 1984

Dear Birthmother:

My adoptive father stopped by my house earlier tonight on his way home from a business trip. During the course of our conversation, I mentioned that I had called the adoption agency to inquire about searching for you. I never thought my dad would feel threatened—even mildly—by my decision to search for you, nor did I expect to have such an emotionally charged dialogue with him about my adoption and the reasons why I want to find you.

He left a couple of hours ago. Now that I look back on our conversation, I'm both happy and relieved that he and I have been able to talk openly and honestly about our feelings regarding my desire to search for you. I'm reassured that I'll have his love and support throughout my search for you. He's reassured that my need to find you in no way affects my relationship with him, nor is it a reflection of my unhappiness with my childhood circumstances (for which, sadly, he takes far too much responsibility, considering the circumstances that were totally out of his control, such as Margery's drinking).

What's most important to me now is that my conversation with him not only happened but also happened in a way that ended well, in spite of the shaky beginning.

When I first mentioned to my father that I had contacted the adoption agency to learn the procedures to find you, he immediately demanded: "What do you want to find her for?"

I started to explain about the need for my medical history, but he interrupted me. He thought my decision to search for you was a result of the difficult relationship my mother Sonja and I had had since she came into my life when I was seven years old—a relationship in which we constantly struggled but failed to reach a satisfying balance in our mother–daughter interactions, much to my father's great disappointment.

"Sonja has raised you and taken care of you in the best way she knew how," he informed me. "I know you two haven't gotten along very well. But I know she loves you very much. What has this other woman done for you? She left your care to other people because she couldn't take care of you."

"I know that, Dad," I replied. "But I'm not searching for my birthmother so that I can find someone else to take care of me."

"I know you haven't had the happiest of childhoods," he continued as if he hadn't heard me. "First Margery and her drinking, and then the foster home, and then you and Mom not getting along—"

"Dad, searching for my birthmother has nothing to do with my childhood," I interrupted. "Or Margery. Or Mom. They aren't the reasons why I want to look for my birthmother. I don't want a 'new' mother or a mother I never had. The fact of the matter is, I don't know if I'll be able to find my birthmother or even whether I'll continue the search after I begin it. So, finding a mother is not what my search is all about."

"Then why would you want to find this woman?"

"It's not so much the *person* I want to find as the *answers* to my questions. I want to find my roots. I want to know where I came from. I want to know my medical history. I want to know my nationality. I want to know why I was placed for adoption. I want to learn the answers to questions that you can't answer, Dad, questions that only my birthmother can answer."

For the next few moments, we were silent. I looked at my dad and wondered what he was thinking. I thought he might be considering what I had just said, about what he couldn't give me: the truth about my past. My father dislikes not being able to do something; he likes to think that anything is possible, no matter what the circumstances. So I wondered whether he was upset that he couldn't give me information I needed about my past.

But I was wrong.

"What about your birthfather?" he had finally asked.

"What about him?"

"Do you want to find him?"

"No," I answered quickly, then thought for a moment. "Well—to tell you the truth, Dad, I hadn't even considered looking for him; it never crossed my mind. I guess my birthmother can give me his name and information about him if and when I find her. But it's my birthmother I really want to find. She's the one who decided to give me up. She's the one who carried me for nine months. It's the mother–daughter bond I think I lost in being adopted. I don't feel I lost a father–daughter connection. If I were a man, maybe I'd feel differently. Maybe I'd want to find my birthfather. I don't know. But you, well . . . you're my . . . well, I know you *really* aren't— we both *know* you really aren't—but as far as I'm concerned, you've always been my *real* father. And you always will be. So I don't need to find my birthfather. I just want to find my birthmother."

My father didn't say anything.

"I'm not looking for a father, Dad," I persisted. "I'm not interested in my birthfather. *He* doesn't matter to me. But my birthmother does."

"I don't want to lose you," my father then said softly.

"Oh, Dad, you're not going to lose me." I moved next to where he was sitting and kneeled by the chair. "I don't want another family, another mother, or another father. I just want some answers." I took one of his hands in mine and held it. "Dad, when you were growing up, you didn't wonder where you came from. Your parents told you. You didn't create fantasies in your mind about why your real parents didn't want you. Your real parents wanted you. When you needed answers and explanations about yourself or when you wanted to hear your family's history, you had the source to ask. I didn't. I still don't. *But that's not your fault.* That's just the way it is, because I'm adopted. Do you understand?"

As I waited for him to reply, I recalled that all my life—except for a few months—he had been there for me. Before that, he had spent ten years loving an alcoholic and trying to make their love work. He had watched his dreams of having a happy, healthy family swept away in a river of alcohol. He had continued to manage his family's business while, at the same time, took on the responsibility of being a single parent at a time when single fathers weren't the norm. And, through it all, he had done his best to think of me first as he provided me with a mother and a warm, comfortable home.

His image wavered in front of me as my eyes watered; tears spilled down my cheeks. At that moment, I wasn't crying for myself or for my own pain, but for the sensitive, loving, kind father who had devoted his life to me. I thought to myself, "Despite the circumstances of your childhood, Amy, you've been blessed by having this gentle man as your father. His main goal has been to do anything he could to make sure you were taken care of."

I said aloud, "You know, Dad, I may have lost my birthmother and Margery and some childhood years, but I've gained the best father I could have possibly had. You've always been there for me. I love you, Dad."

"I love you, too," he replied as he squeezed my hand. "I just wish I could make everything better for you."

"You already have, Dad, just by being there for me." I threw my arms around him and hugged him. In his arms, I felt safe and secure—a child protected—but also young and vulnerable. I began to think about all the emotions about my adoption and my childhood that I had been dealing with since August. I didn't want them to come out. I didn't want them to have free rein, to take over until I became a blubbering child that my dad would want to take care of once again, as he had taken care of me all my life. I wanted to stop the emotions, to stop the tears, because I didn't want him to see me as a needy child anymore. But, with my father holding me, all the feelings I had held in for thirty-one years about being adopted cried out for recognition.

So, in the safety of my father's love, I let them be heard. As the tears spilled out, I told him everything—all the things I've already shared with you in my letters—about growing up adopted and about my childhood.

He held me and just listened.

Then, when my sobs turned into deep sighs and I dried my tears, he gently pulled me away from him and looked into my eyes. It was then I saw that his eyes were misty.

"Oh, Dad, I didn't want to make you cry."

He gave me a quick smile, then said, "I always thought everything was okay for you, Amy, that you were happy. I thought that once you had a home and a mother and a father, everything would be okay, that you would be set for the rest of your life. But now I see that you *do* need to find out certain things about yourself. When you're a kid, I don't think you need to know such things. I don't think it's a good idea to tell anyone that young a lot of details about another mother and father because they might not be ready for the information. Also, it could damage some of the bonding that's needed in the adoptive family.

"But when you're older, as you are now, I think that if you want to, you should be able to find out things about yourself. Especially your medical history. When we adopted you, the agency said that you were healthy and your parents were healthy. But that's not enough to go on today. What with cancer and so many other diseases that run in a family, you need to know *all* your family's medical history. If you run the risk of some disease, you might benefit from medical help now. Your health is important to me. I certainly wouldn't want anything to happen to you that could have been prevented if you had only had information you needed."

"I feel the same way," I said. "I'd also feel a lot better

being able to write something other than 'I don't know' on a medical form."

He nodded.

I breathed a deep sigh and stood up to stretch my legs. "What about the rest of the things I've told you, Dad, like wanting to know where I came from and who I came from? How do you feel about my need to find those things out?"

"I think that if they're important for you to know, you need to do what you can to find your answers. But keep in mind if you find your birthmother, that you may not like *who* you find."

I thought for a moment about what he said. "To be honest, I haven't considered how I'll *feel* about my birthmother. I don't know if it's important whether I like her or dislike her. As I've said, it's not the person I'm as interested in right now as much as the information about my medical history, about not knowing my origins, and about her giving me up."

"She could give you up again, you know," he warned. "Turn her back on you. She may not be a stable person, either. Who knows the reasons why she gave you up. She could be a kook."

I smiled at one of my father's favorite words. "Well, I never thought of the possibility that she might be a kook, Dad. I'd hate to find that out, especially since that might mean I'm a kook, too—genetically speaking, that is. Believe me, I'd rather have the genes of someone I know and trust—like you or Mom—than someone I know nothing about."

"Well, if you're a kook, I'll still love you."

47

"Thanks, Dad. That's just the reassurance I need right now."

We laughed. Then he stood up to leave.

"So, what's next?" he asked as he put on his coat.

"Making an appointment with a case worker at the agency."

"When are you going to do that?"

"I don't know. Whenever I'm ready, but I don't know what it'll take to make me *feel* ready. I think this talk has helped. And, if I know that you'll support me in my decision to find my birthmother, if I know that you'll be there to listen to me and offer me advice when I need it, then maybe that'll give me the strength and courage to make the telephone call."

"I'll support you in any way I can," he replied as he buttoned his coat. "I don't want you to be hurt. I don't want to lose you. And I know Sonja doesn't want to lose you, either."

"You're not going to lose me," I reassured him. "I'm not going anywhere. I'm just looking for some answers. I don't want anything or anyone else. You're my dad and Sonja's my mom. Those things will never change, nor do I want them to."

I kissed my dad good-bye after he told me he'd talk to Sonja about our conversation when he got home. I watched him get into his car, then waved to him from the living room window as he drove away.

Then, as I replayed the conversation I had just had with him in my head, I sat down to write you this letter.

I realize now that I feel relieved that he and I talked, even though I hadn't planned it and hadn't thought about it at all. I think I imagined that I'd tell him and Sonja *after* I knew what the outcome of my search would be. I didn't see the point of preparing them for something that might not happen. After all, who knows whether or not I'll find you?

But I think that now—*before* I know any outcomes—is a better time to talk about the search. My father, as a parent, is more concerned with the feelings that helped me reach this decision to find you. These feelings involve him and my relationship with him. So they're important for us to deal with together, adoptive parent to adoptive child.

But, if/when I find you, what happens between you and me involves us, not my dad. Those feelings will involve our relationship with each other. They'll be up to us to process together, birthmother to birth child.

October 12, 1984

Dear Birthmother:
I called Sonja this morning to ask her if Dad had told her about my decision to search for you. He had.

"How do you feel about what I want to do?" I had asked her.

"Fine," she replied.

"You don't have a problem with it?"

"No."

"Are you sure you're not hurt or threatened or angry?"

"No, no, and no."

Silence filled the telephone lines for a moment.

Then my mother spoke. "Amy, I know why you need to do this."

"You do?"

"Well, I probably shouldn't say it like that. I guess I *think* I know why."

"Why?"

"Well, because you want to put your past to rest. Am I right?"

"Well, I want to find my birthmother because I want to know my medical history and because I'd like to know—"

"Dad told me all that," she interrupted. "But I think the bottom line is that you want to put your past to rest. As long as you're always wondering about what went on years ago, your past is alive; it's in the present. To put it to rest, you have to deal with it and then move away from it. Then you can get on with your life in the present."

Perhaps Sonja was able to be more objective because she was neither my biological nor my adoptive mother. Maybe she was more astute than I was at assessing my need to find a connection in my life after such a disconnected past. Maybe she was more practical than either my dad or I could ever be, with our emotions so tied to each other and to our pasts.

But, for whatever the reason, Sonja had very neatly, very

succinctly, and very accurately assessed my need to find you in a nutshell.

I want to find you so I can put my past to rest.

October 16, 1984

Dear Birthmother:
I've been thinking about my conversation with Sonja for the past few days.

I realize now that in that one short telephone conversation, she and I had achieved a rare glimmer of a mother–daughter bond. She showed me that she understood me and how I was feeling in a way that my father couldn't quite fully grasp. Yet, despite the fact that Sonja and I aren't close, she was able to connect with me in the way I believe only a mother can.

I wonder now: Is part of the reason I want to search for you a desire to experience some sort of mother–daughter interaction—one I didn't have with Margery; one that was not only temporary but also not required with my foster mother, Mom Fowler; and one that, up to this point in time, hasn't been achieved with Sonja?

Will you and I be able to connect as a mother and daughter without knowing much about each other?

Is a mother–daughter connection something that's developed, over time, or is it something very natural that neither time nor circumstance can disconnect?

October 21, 1984

Dear Mother Person:

I may have found an answer to the final question in my last letter to you. Here it is: I think the mother–daughter connection is a very natural one, which neither time nor circumstance can disconnect.

I base this conclusion on some things I learned about Margery in 1976, when I also sadly learned that she had died in November 1975 in a fire in her home.

I wouldn't have heard about her death if she hadn't left me part of her estate. Her lawyers sent me a copy of the will in early 1976, when they settled her estate. I remember at the time how taken aback I had been to read: "To my daughter, Amy Elizabeth Dean. . . . " I couldn't understand why she still thought of me as her daughter, since she hadn't seen me since I was three and had had no contact with either me or my father.

But when I wrote to Mom Fowler that year about Margery's death (Mom Fowler and I have kept in touch by mail and through brief visits a few times a year), what I received in response from her gave me the reason why Margery still thought of me as her daughter after all those years.

Mom Fowler sent me a letter Margery had written to her in 1956, when the Fowlers were appointed to take care of me. In rereading her carefully composed, handwritten letter once again today, it's clear to me that Margery still

52

considered me her daughter up to her death because *she was my mother*. And nothing—not divorce, not losing custody of me, not being able to see me, and not the disease of alcoholism—could change that for her.

Her letter is a testimony to me of her mother's love and her mother's knowledge of me, as a baby, that no one else had—not you, not Mom Fowler, and not Sonja. Hers are the words of a mother who loved her child and who, because of the mother–daughter connection, never stopped loving her.

Dear Mrs. Fowler:
<u>PLAY</u>
This may be a jumble to you, as I am writing as things come to mind. Amy is very easy to get along with. She is a wonderful child and plays very well by herself, although she loves other kids. She likes to play with "money" (change), playing cards, or for that matter, cards of any kind, such as tags, greeting cards, etc. I hope you or someone near you has a sandbox. She'll spend hours there. She will talk to you about "going to the beach in the summer and playing in the sand." She is very anxious to go, and we hope we can take her soon.

She likes books and likes to be read to.

She likes to play hide 'n go seek and ride piggyback.

She likes to make mud pies, play "Betty Crocker" (also likes to help you bake).

Loves the Mickey Mouse Club on TV (practically a must). Also Gary Moore and the noontime serials. Lots of times I let her play with her cups (in the basket) in soap suds in the sink after the dishes are done and I'm cleaning up the kitchen.

Likes to play records.

Loves it outdoors, but she's a wanderer.

Likes to "write" on paper with pencils, also likes to paint.

Calls pencils "writes."

TOILET

If constipated, I give her a teaspoon of Castoria.

She wears diapers (a double one and training pants at night). Otherwise she's very good. Wears training pants all day. She will tell you when she has to go to the "John."

No. 1—she calls Trickle.

No. 2—is making a "mess."

Sometimes she wants you to stay with her, sometimes she'd rather be alone.

Her buttocks is her "PO PO." When naughty, you're going to spank her PO PO.

SLEEP

Eats lunch around noon and watches the TV serials (*Valiant Lady, Love of Life, Search for Tomorrow,* and *Guiding Light*). She goes to bed about 1:00 P.M. Usually "fools around" for a while, so you may have to go in and tell her "no more fooling around." Usually sleeps or is quiet 2½ hours. (Of course, there are days she won't go to sleep but plays very well in her room.) Goes to bed at 8:00 P.M. and watches the cars out the window and the stars and moon, etc. You may have to go up two or three times for a big kiss and a big hug and a "See ya later alligator . . . See ya around fox hound . . . After awhile crocodile," or another "milk 'n. . . . "

If you have a rocking chair, she likes "rocka, rocka" at night and will sing "Rockabye Baby."

Her daddy puts her to bed at night.

She wakes up between 6:30 and 7:00 A.M.

FOOD

Amy is not a very good eater. Lives on vitamins, milk, chocolate eggnogs (one every night), and oranges. However, besides these she likes

Woody's Chuck o'Good Cheddar Cheese

hamburgers	V-8 Vegetable Juice	corn flakes
hot dogs	pineapple juice	ice cream
chicken	fish	bacon

Junior Foods (pears, peaches, and pineapple)

whipped cream	boiled or baked potato	corn
potato chips	Oreo cream sandwiches	peas

I hope you can get her to eat more.

Amy likes all kinds of animals, dogs especially, but also cats, birds, and bugs of all kinds.

She likes to go "bye bye" in the car.

Is interested in all that goes on around her.

We think she talks very well, and you can talk to her too. She seems to understand everything.

She has a shampoo with Halo every Sunday morning in the bathtub. She will show you how she "tips back" so the soap won't get in her eyes.

Amy is a very good girl. Please give her lots of love.

We will miss her so much.

Very sincerely,

Margery and Bruce Dean

P.S. She also loves to go "shopping" at the grocery store. (She knows where everything is.)

Dear Birthmother:

I always feel sad and depressed whenever I reread Margery's letter. I feel sad for her. I can't tell from the letter whether Margery thought my relocation was a temporary measure or a more permanent one. I assume Margery believed (as do most alcoholics) that she would soon be better and that I would be coming home to her. But there's an air of melancholy and a sense of hopelessness that comes through in her writing that suggests she might have known she wouldn't see me again.

I wonder: Did you ever experience such feelings in giving me up?

later, October 25

Dear First Mother:

I've been thinking more about Margery's letter and about you.

I wonder: How do you feel about what she said? Did what she wrote convey what it might have been like for you—or for any mother—to give up her daughter—her flesh and blood—to the care of someone else? Would it have been painful for you to write such a letter—to be forced to think about the important things about your baby that you wished to convey to another caretaker; to trust that your baby would be loved and nurtured and not want for anything?

Maybe I'm right in my assumptions about a mother—daughter bond: that the bond a mother has with her child isn't strengthened so much by time, events, or memories. It's strengthened more by experiences such as carrying the child, delivering the child, taking care of the child, or feeling some degree of protection and love for the child.

October 29, 1984

Dear Birthmother:

I wonder, if I had contact with Margery today, whether she would accept the news of my desire to search for you with as much clarity, knowledge, and agreeability as Sonja has?

If Margery's drinking and the foster home had never happened and my adoptive parents were still together, would she object to my search or be highly threatened?

Given such circumstances, would my dad even want to give me his support?

November 2, 1984

Dear Mother from the Past:

I'm afraid that if I don't begin the search for you soon,

when I'm in my thirties and you're (probably?) in your fifties, death might once again take a mother from me.

But now I wonder:

What if you're already dead?

I've made the decision to search for you because I want to meet you, to see you, to connect with you in some way.

But what if you're not alive? What if I *can't* connect with you? What do I do then?

Until now, I've assumed that you're alive. But you could have been sickly and died shortly after you gave birth to me. (However, I'd still need to "find" you in case your cause of death could have been genetically passed along to me.) You could have died when I was a child and left me an orphan (as I've considered in one of my reason-for-my-adoption theories). Or you could have died sometime after you placed me for adoption.

If you're not alive, what do I do with all the emotions I have about you and about my adoption?

Will these feelings die with you?

November 4, 1984

Dear Unknown Woman:

What if you're an alcoholic as Margery was? Or a drug addict? Or a prostitute?

What if you're a bag lady? What if you wear frumpy

clothes and far too much makeup, and drink constantly and chain smoke and talk too loudly?

What happens if *you're* my mother?

November 6, 1984

Dear Woman from Long Ago:
What if you're famous and don't want anyone to know about me? What if you view me as someone who could ruin your career or your life?

What if you offered me a large sum of money to keep quiet about the fact that you're my mother? Would I take the money? Or would I simply walk away from you and do what you ask of me—keep quiet?

November 7, 1984

Dear Birthmother:
What if you've been waiting all these years to be reunited with me, as most of the fairy-tale-come-true adoption search stories in the popular women's magazines claim birthmothers do?

What if you're puttering in your kitchen right now, glancing from time to time at the telephone on the wall, wondering when it will ring and a voice will inform you that your daughter would like to say hello to you?

What if you want to make me part of your life? What if

you have a husband and children but want me to be part of your family, too?

What if you want to reclaim your flesh and blood?

I've been so worried about how you might reject me if/when I find you.

But I've never even considered how I'd feel if you welcomed me with open arms.

November 11, 1984

Dear Woman Who I'm Ready to Find:

As of today, all the "what-ifs" I could ever possibly conjure up about you are being put to rest.

I've made the decision to call the adoption agency after the holidays are over (I think the holiday season is hectic and emotional enough without adding more to it).

For now, and until the first of the year, I plan on concentrating less on outcomes with you and more on living my own life a day at a time.

Then, when 1985 is new, I'll honor my New Year's resolution: to do everything I need to do to find you.

During the Search

One does not bury the past; one lives with it.
—MAY SARTON
The Small Room

The "adoption triangle" of child, birthparents, and adoptive parents has traditionally been one of the most secret relationships in American life.
—Arthur Kroeber,
contributing reporter, *Boston Globe*

January 1, 1985

Dear Birthmother:

Happy New Year for me, for you—for us?!?

Today I need to keep in mind Ralph Waldo Emerson's words about taking risks as I stay true to my resolution to soon begin the process of searching for you:

"Do not be too timid and squeamish about your actions. All life is an experiment."

I think that while most experiments are often termed successful or unsuccessful, depending on their outcomes, very few experiments are termed "a waste of time" or something that "should never have been done."

So, what Emerson's words mean to me are that any

61

experiment in life that's undertaken *has* to be considered worthwhile in some measure, no matter what the results, simply because of what it teaches.

I don't know what I'll find, if/when I find you, but the results aren't as important as what I may learn.

Looking for you is an *experiment*; what happens after that is my *experience*.

January 9, 1985

Dear Birthmother:

Today I opened a letter at work, addressed to me from the president of the company. The letter began:

Dear Amy:

It is with deep regret that Parker Brothers must announce a layoff that will become effective January 11, 1985, and unfortunately, you are affected. ...

Although this news wasn't unexpected—the company has had a few layoffs previous to this one, and it was common knowledge, both within the industry and within the company, that the company wasn't doing well—there was a small part of me that held on to the belief that I was too valuable, too hard a worker, too important, too well liked, too nice a person—too *whatever*—to be let go.

I thought that the company wouldn't let go of me simply because I was me.

But company layoffs rarely deal with individual personalities. They focus on numbers—profits and losses, products and sales, facts and figures.

Parker Brothers was no different.

And Amy Dean was just a number to them, not a personality.

Today I was a person caught in a circumstance over which I had no control.

January 15, 1985

Dear Birthmother:

I just reread my last letter to you. I'm amazed at how the last line jumps out at me now:

"*. . . I was a person caught in a circumstance over which I had no control.*"

Although I haven't written that sentence to you in any previous letter, I believe that's what I've been relating to you all along—that I feel like a person who has been caught in a series of events that affect me but that I cannot change, that I cannot control. This sense of powerlessness started with being adopted and has extended to include other circumstances in my life as well.

For example, I couldn't say to you years ago: "Hey, lady, don't let me go! We'll make it okay. You'll see."

I couldn't say to Margery: "Put the damn bottle down and be my mother."

I couldn't say to my dad: "Please take me out of this

foster home, get Margery to stop drinking, and let's get back to being a family."

I couldn't say to Sonja: "Come on—it's up to you now to make everything right for me."

Since the day I was born, decisions have been made that concern me, that are for me, and that are about me, but I've had no freedom to input my feelings or my thoughts about any decision or its outcome.

Now that I've been laid off, I'm once again powerless. I didn't have any input in the decision. The company didn't ask me how I would feel if I was laid off. The company doesn't ask me now how I feel. I can't change the company's mind. The decision has been made. I'm out. And that's it.

I can't change it.

January 19, 1985

Dear Birthmother:

Remember what I wrote to you in an earlier letter, about how the losses in my life build up, one on top of the other, beginning with my original loss of you as my mother?

Often I feel the same way in situations where I'm powerless. My adoption was the original loss of power. The fallout from Margery's drinking was next. Staying in the foster home followed. Then the divorce of my adoptive parents.

Just as the losses in my life overwhelm me, so too do

the situations where I'm powerless. I can't keep them in perspective; I can't deal with each one as it occurs.

Instead, like my losses, they pile up, one on top of the other, until it seems as if all I've experienced in my life since Day One have been situations in which I cannot be heard, I cannot be considered, I cannot be felt, I cannot make an impact—*where I am powerless.*

January 25, 1985

Dear Birthmother:

I had a dream last night about the "piles" of losses and powerlessness in my life. In my dream, it was summer and I was camping at one of my favorite campsites in Vermont. I was collecting firewood to build a fire. I scoured the woods and carried great piles of dry wood to the clearing. Then I began stacking the wood in position in a box-triangle fire formation I had learned to build at summer camp.

The small fire I was constructing to cook my dinner grew larger and larger. But I didn't stop piling sticks on the fire formation as it grew. Instead, I rose from a kneeling position and placed the sticks from a standing position. Soon I was reaching up and placing sticks on top of the pile that was now above my head.

But I still didn't stop building. I ran back to the woods and dragged out small dead trees to add to the pile. My fire formation grew to the size of a bonfire.

Exhausted, I finally struck a match and lit the base of the sticks. They immediately burst into flame. It wasn't long before there was a wall of flames in front of me.

I remember thinking, either in my dream or in a semiconscious, dream-reality state, "The fire's going to rage out of control and burn down the campground. When that happens, I won't be allowed to camp here anymore. The park rangers will tell me they don't want me to come back."

But that thought only made me angry. Rather than try to extinguish the fire, I charged into the woods. I frantically wrapped my arms around each tree I came to, lifted it out of the ground, and dragged it back to the fire, where I raised it high above my head and tossed it on the inferno, sending red hot sparks flying in all directions.

I leveled the forest until there were no trees left, and then I let the fire burn out of control.

When it was over—when there was nothing left but several blackened stumps and a thick haze of smoke that hung in the air—a wave of relief washed over me and extinguished the last spark of frustration that burned within me.

I imagine this dream symbolizes the powerlessness I feel about being laid off, about one more "stick" being added to the "powerlessness pile" that has been building all my life.

But while I'm powerless to get my job back or to change any event that happened to me as a child, I do have the power to search for you.

That is in my control.

January 31, 1985

Dear Birthmother:

I called the adoption agency a couple of hours ago and made an appointment for February 21, about three weeks from now. It was the first time I could get in because of the case worker's schedule and the job interviews and freelance work I've scheduled.

My case worker's name is Mary Ann.

The address of the agency is 21 Cedar Street in Worcester. The agency gave me directions because I wasn't sure where Cedar Street was.

The telephone call was brief.

After I hung up the phone, I paced around my house for several minutes.

I wished I was at work.

I wished I was doing something that would help me take my mind off the upcoming wait of 21 days, 504 hours, 30,240 minutes, and 1,814,400 seconds (figuring the time out on a calculator did distract me for a bit!).

I feel nervous even though the appointment is a few weeks away.

I wonder: What should I wear?

February 6, 1985

Dear Birthmother:

What if I say something *wrong* when I meet with Mary Ann, something that will make her decide that I shouldn't search for you?

Should I tell her about my childhood? Should I let her know that Margery was an alcoholic? If I do, will she think that I'm blaming or criticizing the agency for not recognizing that Margery was an alcoholic when they let her adopt me?

February 13, 1985

Dear Birthmother:

There's only one week left!

I've decided to tell Mary Ann whatever she wants to know about me, about how I feel, and about what happened to me after I was placed for adoption. I'm not going to hide anything from her or lie.

For what would be the point? In looking for you, I want to uncover the answers, to find out the truth.

So I plan to be open and honest with Mary Ann about everything.

Dear Birthmother:

My first meeting with Mary Ann is over. It wasn't long; it lasted perhaps thirty to forty minutes.

Mary Ann first asked me a lot of questions about myself and my life. I told her everything, from what happened after I was adopted to my reasons for wanting to find you.

Then she asked me about my present-day relationships—family, friends, and others. She told me she needed to know what kind of emotional support I have in my life because finding a biological parent can be a disruptive and emotional experience. She let me know that it was important for me to have people I can talk to, who can help me through any difficult times I might encounter in searching for you.

I detailed my close relationship with my adoptive father and my last conversation with Sonja, as well as let her know that I had an understanding and supportive lover and a therapist who was familiar with my background.

Toward the end of our meeting, she asked me if I wanted to find you.

"Yes," I tried to respond with as much patience and calmness in my voice as I could muster because I was thinking, "*Of course* I want to find my birthmother. Isn't that why I'm here?"

"Then I'll meet with the director and a decision will be made in a couple of days on whether to proceed to the next step, which is providing you with nonidentifying information."

"Oh," I replied. I knew she must have heard the disappointment in my voice because she raised an eyebrow.

"I guess, well, I guess I thought we'd do everything today," I explained, then smiled. "But I've been thinking seriously about this—well, *obsessing* is a better word—since last August. You've just met me. Of course, you need time to assess the situation. I'm sorry. I'm just a little impatient."

"That's understandable," she replied. "But it's important that I know you'll be okay with information you're given and with finding your birthmother, if we can locate her.

"How well you're going to handle this is what's important to me and to the agency."

February 22, 1985

Dear Birthmother:

Today was a long day. Even though Mary Ann said she'd call in a couple of days with the agency's decision, I jumped every time the phone rang.

I don't know what I'll do if the agency decides not to help me with the search. Should I take a negative response as an indication that I may not be emotionally ready to find you? Or should I just proceed with a search on my own? I could try to find you myself. Or I could hire a detective to help me. I wonder how expensive that would be. Could a lawyer help me?

I can't believe how impatient I feel. I haven't tried to find you for thirty years. Now every minute that passes seems like precious moments of time that are wasted.

February 23, 1985

Dear Birthmother:

Mary Ann called today to tell me that the agency will help me contact you!

So the next step is to see Mary Ann again in a few days. At that time, she'll give me nonidentifying information about you.

I'm so excited!

I can't wait to learn more about you!

February 28, 1985

Dear Birthmother:

When I met with Mary Ann in her office earlier today, she opened a folder and handed me a sheet of paper with the following nonidentifying information about you and me on it. I sat in a chair across the room from her and read what she had given to me:

Birthmother (Methodist)
Eighteen-year-old woman staying with relatives in

Worcester County; planned to return after baby's birth to other state with mother and older sister. Parents divorced when mother was young; father remarried.

Referred by physician; had come to area in summer following high school graduation to deliver the baby and release for adoption.

Had concealed pregnancy for six months; mother was supportive.

Social worker comments a month prior to baby's birth about birthmother: ". . . is an attractive girl, probably 5'6" or 5'7" tall, well built, sandy-colored hair, medium light complexion, an outgoing personality." Scottish, English, Irish descent.

Gave following information about birthfather: 25 years old, married, not aware of pregnancy; Italian descent; good health. Employed as a draftsman.

Baby: Linda Joan (not seen by mother)
DOB: 10/3/53
7 lb 9 oz "normal, healthy, well-developed baby" 19½ in.

Decision to release baby was always a firm one and supported by relatives with whom she stayed. Mother's mother (maternal grandmother) also signed assent form for surrender.

Baby to foster home on 10/8/53.

1/5/54: *Baby's developmental exam, age 3 months*
". . . well developed, good social responses, excellent interest and drive. She shows a certain vigor in her approach and her entire performance was well

integrated. . . . She should be placed with a family wishing a girl with 'a lot of get up and go.'"

2/15/54: Preplacement visit with Deans, who were "immediately taken by this baby. . . ."

2/19/54: Placement made with Deans.

I looked at Mary Ann after I had finished reading the information. She asked me if I had any questions.

I didn't reply for a few moments, then shook my head. "No questions. At least, not now. I'm so . . . I don't know . . . ." I glanced down at the piece of paper, which appeared to be trembling as I held it in a slightly shaky hand. I cleared my throat. "There's so much here. It's . . . it's only a sheet of paper, but there's . . . *so much*."

Mary Ann smiled in understanding. "Many people feel exactly the way you do, Amy. There's a lot to digest. Some adoptees I've met with take this information home and just sit with it for a while."

I nodded, then noticed I was sitting on the edge of my seat. I slid back in the chair, then stared at the floor.

After a minute of silence, Mary Ann asked, "How do you feel about what you've read?"

I shrugged my shoulders and met her eyes. "I don't know how I feel right now. I don't know what to think. I don't know what to say."

"That's okay. Give yourself some time."

I nodded, then asked, "May I have a copy of this?"

"That's yours to keep."

"Thanks."

I stared at Mary Ann and shifted position in the chair. I felt hot. I felt uncomfortable.

"Amy, what do you think you'd like to do next?" she asked. "Would you like to proceed with the search? I have some good leads for locating your birthmother. Or would you like to take this information home and think about your next step for a while?"

I thought for a few moments. What was my answer? My mind was a jumbled mass of thoughts; none of them was clear. I prodded myself by silently asking: "Come on, Amy, what do you want?"

In response, what came to mind was leaving—no, escaping from—Mary Ann's office. I suddenly felt suffocated and claustrophobic. I imagined running out of her office, jumping in my car, and driving home as fast as I could—home to safety, home to security, home to serenity.

In my calmest voice I responded: "I'd like to think about what I've found out. I don't want to do anything yet."

Mary Ann nodded. As I left, she said she'd wait to hear from me.

March 2, 1985

Dear Birthmother:
I don't know if I want to try to find you.

Before I left her office, Mary Ann reassured me that most adoptees feel overwhelmed after they receive their nonidentifying information. They often experience feelings of confusion, nervousness, fear, and anxiety.

But I didn't think looking for you would make me feel physically ill. I feel slightly nauseous. I have a splitting headache. I haven't slept or eaten well. I feel edgy.

Mary Ann said some adoptees stop their search after receiving the nonidentifying information because they're satisfied with having information they've never had before.

I don't know if I'm satisfied knowing things about you (and about me) that I didn't know before. I feel guilty for opening up information that has been closed for so many years. I feel like a grave robber, violating facts that you believed you had put to rest—had buried in your heart and in your mind—long ago.

Mary Ann told me that some adoptees wait a long time before giving the go-ahead to proceed with the search.

Maybe that's what I should do. I don't know.

March 4, 1985

Dear Birthmother:

Do you realize that *not once* have I ever considered that you were a teenager when you gave birth to me?

All along, I think I've subconsciously imagined you to be the kind of mother I've always dreamed of having—

...a kindly woman with a sweet, smiling face who

gently washes away the dirt from my scraped knees and elbows and who chases away my tears;

. . . a tireless woman who provides me with soft, clean clothing that smells a little like her and a little like the fresh outdoors;

. . . a caring woman who does many things with me, who talks with me and shows an interest in my life;

. . . a nurturing woman who makes the house smell as scrumptious as a home-baked cookie and who never lets me know what hunger feels like;

. . . an angelic woman who makes me feel safe as she takes me in her arms, places my head gently upon her soft, full bosom, and rocks me to sleep each night.

I never once imagined my mother to be an unmarried teenager who had just graduated from high school, who carried a child in secrecy and left her home state to give birth, then gave up this child—*without even seeing her*—to return home.

I never once imagined that this could be you.

But now that I know the truth, I think I've been naive not to have ever considered the possibility that I was an illegitimate child and that you were, in many ways, a child yourself when you gave birth to me.

March 5, 1985

Dear Birthmother:

Today, when I woke up, I wondered how you felt thirty-one years ago, waking up in your own bedroom and knowing you were pregnant. How did you handle it? How did you conceal your pregnancy for six months? How did you hold such an intimate secret inside for so long?

Did you wake up each morning and remind yourself that no one could learn your terrible secret? Did you go to sleep at night relieved that another day had passed without anyone finding out?

As I lay in bed this morning thinking about you, I began to cry. I felt sad inside, sad for the eighteen-year-old woman/child who may have found herself facing the world each day as a different person.

Were you scared? Lonely? Ashamed? Unhappy?

My heart aches now to know how you felt.

My heart goes out to you.

March 6, 1985

Dear Birthmother:

Maybe, if I found you, I could be a support to you. I could comfort you. I could reassure you. I could let you know that I'm okay.

March 7, 1985

Dear Birthmother:

I realized tonight that whether you wanted to or not, you

had to give me up for adoption. What else could you have done, given your circumstances?

I imagine that, in 1953, there weren't many reputable physicians or clinics that you could have gone to for a safe abortion. The man you had been with was married and, for whatever reasons, you felt that you couldn't tell him of your dilemma.

So you were forced to bring me to term, to carry me for nine months. But since you were an unmarried eighteen-year-old in 1953, when young, single mothers and day care centers weren't the norm, there was no way you could have cared for me as my mother.

So you had no other choice: You *had* to place me for adoption.

But I'd like to know how you felt about that, how you felt when you knew that you had to give me up.

March 8, 1985

Dear Birthmother:

I just remembered one of the things Mary Ann told me during my first meeting with her. She stated that she wanted to be sure I could handle a search for you.

I wonder now: Can *you* handle my search for you? Or will contact with me bring back painful memories?

March 9, 1985

Dear Birthmother:

I think about the twenty-five-year-old married man who was my father and wonder: Did you love him? Had he made you promises, perhaps told you that he would leave his wife for you? Did you imagine that you had a future with him?

Or did he take advantage of you? Did he force you to do something that you didn't want to do?

Did you regret the act that made you pregnant with me, or did you do it out of love?

March 10, 1985

Dear Birthmother:

Are you happy now?

Or are you haunted, from time to time, by the memories of your past?

March 12, 1985

Dear Birthmother:

Perhaps if I found you, I might discover that adoptees may

not be the only ones who experience feelings of loss and powerlessness. Perhaps those who place children for adoption feel those feelings just as acutely. Am I right in this assumption?

When I wrote to you in an earlier letter about loss, I wondered if you knew what it was like to lose. But perhaps you know, more than I do, what loss is all about. You lost at least nine months (if not more, depending on how my birth and the adoption affected you) from your teenage years of innocence and joy when you faced the responsibility and gravity of your pregnancy at a time when such a mature dilemma shouldn't have even been a factor. You may have lost some respect from your friends or family who knew of your condition. You may have lost some degree of self-respect. You may have lost your sense of security by living in another state with relatives until you gave birth to me.

Finally, depending on how you felt about me, you may have believed that you lost a child you cared for when you had to give me up.

You may also know quite well what I was talking about in my recent letters, about how it feels to be powerless, how it feels to be ". . . a person caught in a circumstance, over which (you have) no control." Your unplanned pregnancy at the age of eighteen certainly falls into the realm of powerlessness. But such feelings could have begun even before that, with the twenty-five-year-old married man who was my father. Maybe you loved him and would have done anything for him. Or maybe you felt you had no choice but to give him what he wanted from you.

And, six months into your pregnancy, when your secret was finally known, you may have been powerless in the decision making about what would happen to your child after it was born. Maybe you wanted to take care of me and didn't want to give me up. Maybe you tried to verbalize this. But what you may have felt or even said to the adults who were taking care of you might not have mattered. My life may have been in your body, but it may not have been in your control.

I don't know whether I'm right or wrong in these assumptions. But I'd like to think that my adoption may have affected you as well.

March 14, 1985

Dear Birthmother:

I called Mary Ann today to tell her that I wanted to find you.

"I want to know more," I told her. "While I'm happy to find out things about myself and my adoption that I didn't know, and while I'm satisfied to learn that certain information that was given to me when I was growing up was true, like my nationality and my birthname, *it's just not enough*. The nonidentifying information just gives me the facts.

"But I want to know the *feelings*. I want to know how my birthmother felt about her pregnancy and my adoption. I want to know what has happened to her since then. I want to know who she is. I want to find out more.

"So would you try to find her for me?"

April 9, 1985

Dear Birthmother:

Mary Ann called today and said she had made contact with you.

"She's alive!" was my first response.

"Yes, and she lives in Attleboro," Mary Ann told me. I couldn't believe it. Out of all the places in the United States—in the world, for that matter—to live, you end up living less than two hours from me!

"Amy, she wants to talk to you," Mary Ann told me. "Is it all right if I give her your phone number so she can call you?"

"Yes," I said without hesitation, excited to learn that you *wanted* to hear from me.

"Okay. I'm going to call her now, after I hang up with you. As soon as I contact her, she'll probably want to call you. Will you be home?"

"Yes, yes," I quickly responded, urging Mary Ann off the phone.

"Fine. I'll call her now."

As I hung up the phone, I realized that in a few minutes I could be talking to you—the woman who had brought me into the world.

A few minutes later, the phone rang.

My heart pounded as I said, "Hello?"

But the voice that started talking was that of a friend. I interrupted her and asked if I could call her back, then hung up the phone.

I began pacing back and forth from the kitchen to the living room. Minutes ticked by. I sat down on the couch and tried to read a magazine, but immediately stood up and began pacing again.

Almost fifteen minutes went by. Then the phone rang. "Hello?"

It was Mary Ann. "Your birthmother's line has been busy. But I'll keep trying until the agency closes today. If I can't get in touch with her before I leave, I'll call her first thing tomorrow morning."

My heart sank. "Okay, Mary Ann." I knew that the dejection in my voice was apparent. "I'll be waiting."

I hung up the phone and began pacing again. Fifteen minutes passed. Then a half hour.

Exasperated, I went to the refrigerator and took out food to make a salad. I concentrated on washing and breaking the lettuce, chopping carrots and onions, and cutting up fresh vegetables.

Midway into my preparations, the telephone rang.

Without thinking, I reached for the phone, then realized— at the moment the receiver touched my ear—that this could be the call I had been waiting for.

"Hello?" I answered expectantly.

"Amy? This is Ruth. I'm your birthmother. . . ."

After the Search

Not everything that is faced can be changed; but nothing can be changed until it is faced.
—JAMES BALDWIN

The need to know is always there.... It's not so much that you want a relationship with her [your birthmother]; it's more like a little piece of you is missing and you want to find it.
—JIM BIANCO,
a twenty-one-year-old who found his birthparents,
in a *Boston Globe* article by Eileen Kuperschmid

Later, April 9, 1985

Dear Ruth:

We talked to each other—*for the first time*—earlier this afternoon for about an hour. I wish I could remember what the first words were that you said to me after you said hello and identified who you were; I wish, too, that I could recall what I first said to you. I can't remember now. I wasn't focused on the beginning of our conversation because I kept thinking to myself, "This is the woman who gave birth to me. This is the person who I've been longing to find." Feelings bombarded me—I wanted to laugh, to cry, to shout, to be held, to run away.

Our first words are gone now from my memory.

But I have in front of me, as I write this, a piece of paper filled with hastily scribbled notes—notes I took after I recovered from the initial shock of hearing your voice and you asked, "What do you want to know, Amy?"

I wanted to cry out, "Everything!" But I didn't want you to think I was being too pushy or demanding. I wanted to be careful, to not say anything that might make you want to hang up, to reject me, or to be angry with me.

So instead I said, "I'd like to know about my medical history." You promptly filled me in on your medical history and your family's—about the prostate cancer on your father's side and the diabetes on your mother's. "Everyone else is in good health," you commented, then added that you were allergic to some foods. We discovered that we shared a milk allergy, and I jokingly thanked you for depriving me of ice cream.

Then you asked me what I looked like. I remembered how I had longed, all my life, to find a mother who I mirrored in appearance (like the Brady children and their parents). So I described myself to you, hoping that you'd respond, with each piece of information, "Really? That's the same for me, too." But the only thing we had in common was our brown-red, straight hair. Not even our eye color was the same.

"You have your father's eyes," you explained to me. "His eyes were dark, dark brown."

"What else can you tell me about him?" I then asked.

For several moments, you didn't say anything. I thought,

"Now I've done it. I've asked the wrong question, and she won't talk to me anymore."

But then you spoke. In a soft voice you said, "I was raped, Amy."

Now it was my turn to be silent.

"Oh," I finally answered, but I didn't know what else to say. I hadn't considered the possibility that I had been the product of a rape.

You must have been able to read my mind then because you quickly broke into my thoughts: "Amy, even though I was raped—and *that* is a painful memory to me, even after all these years, because he was a friend of the family—*you* weren't a painful memory to me. I never wanted to give you up. But I had to.

"Do you know," you continued, "I wasn't supposed to see you after you were born—so the letting go would be easier, I had been told. But a nurse brought you to me, and I cried when I saw you."

"My case worker told me that you hadn't seen me," I replied.

"Well, she's wrong. I *did* see you. And I'll never forget that, just as I've never forgotten you."

I listened as you continued talking, but my mind began to wander. Sometimes I listened to the sound of your voice and tried to picture what you looked like. Other times I tried to visualize the things you talked about—the rape or seeing me for the first (and what you thought to be the last) time—as if re-creating those moments would bring me closer to my lost years.

"I'm married and have three children," you then related. (I look at my "family notes" now and see that I've written down your children's names and ages.) You told me about your children—where they're living and what they're doing—and you identified them as "your (meaning *my*) brother and sisters." For the first time in our conversation, I felt really uncomfortable. I didn't like to hear you call your children *my* brother and sisters, even though we're related by blood and you're our mother. When I first heard you give them that label, I attributed my discomfort to the fact that I've been an only child all my life; hearing that I had a brother and sisters was therefore foreign to me.

But now I realize that it was at that point in our conversation that we stopped talking about your past and your brief relationship with me and began talking about your/my family: "my" aunts and uncles, "my" grandparents, and "my" cousins. The theme of the conversation had changed; I felt as if you were pulling me into your life *now* and steering us away from what it was like for you (for us) *then*.

But I couldn't tell you that at the time. In fact, when you said, "I want you to know that you're welcome in the family. I've told everyone about you because I wanted to be honest with them. They accept you, Amy. They want to meet you, and so do I," we arranged a time when I could meet you and one of my siblings who lives near you. I wrote down the directions to your house. Then we ended our first conversation by saying, "See you soon."

But as I think now about how I feel, I don't know if I

want to meet your daughter or any other member of your/my family just yet.

I don't know if I'm ready to become part of your life—your family—*in the present*. I think that we have so much more to discuss about our past, that I don't think I'm ready to jump from an initial telephone conversation into a place in your family.

How do I tell you that?

April 11, 1985

Dear Ruth:

Which do you believe is stronger: an emotional bond or a blood bond?

I believe that just because someone is blood related doesn't mean that connection *can't* be broken. Ours was. And just because someone *isn't* blood related doesn't mean that bond can't be even stronger than any blood bond. I believe that my connection with my dad is as strong as, or even stronger than, one I would have with a biological father.

It seems, from our first conversation, that our blood bond means that after thirty-one years—and without any developed emotional attachment—I can be included as a legitimate member of your family, along with those who you've raised, those who have raised you, and those who you've known for most of your life.

But I didn't search for you because I wanted to meet the

members of your family and be accepted by them. In fact, if I had discovered that you weren't alive, I wouldn't then have chosen to search for other members of your family.

It's *you* that I wanted to find, not a family.

Dear Ruth:

You telephoned me today and said you had called one of your/my aunts in Arizona. In your conversation with her, she had asked you for a picture of me.

"Would it be all right if I took some pictures of you when you come to visit?" you asked. "I'd like to send them out to the rest of the family so they know what you look like."

"I don't mind your taking my picture," I responded, "but I don't know how keen I am on having it sent to your relatives."

"*Your* relatives, Amy. These are *your* family members, too."

"I think that's easier for you to say than it is for me, Ruth."

"You'll get used to it over time."

"I don't know if I will. You see—"

"You know, Amy," you interrupted me, "your coming back in my life is so important to me. You were always special to me. I just want everyone to know about you. I love you, Amy."

I was just about to finish what I had been saying, but your last statement rendered me speechless. You continued talking; I responded with one- or two-word answers until we said good-bye.

As I hung up the phone, I felt stunned and confused.

How could you say that you loved me?

You don't even know me—you don't know *anything* about me.

Did you say you loved me because you really do?

Did you say you loved me because that's how you feel, having carried me inside you for nine months and given birth to me?

Did you say you loved me because you feel that's what a mother should say to her child?

Did you say you loved me because you've found me?

Did you say you loved me because one part of that love is guilt over our separation and another part is relief over our reunion?

Just what *is* this love you say you feel for me?

And why don't I feel it for you, too?

April 14, 1985

Dear Ruth:

I realize that I'm the one who opened the door to let you into my life after thirty-one years. I'm the one who contacted the adoption agency. I'm the one who gave Mary

Ann the go-ahead to search for you. I'm the one who gave her permission to give you my telephone number so you could call me.

By these actions, it's only logical that you'd think I'd want to see you right away.

But I don't know if I'm ready to have the door so wide open now.

What would happen if I closed the door to you for just a bit?

April 15, 1985

Dear Ruth:

I called you today to cancel the get-together we had arranged when we first spoke to each other. I feel badly now because I could tell, from the tone of your voice, that you were disappointed. When I tried to explain that I needed a little more time—that I *did* want to see you (but not right away)—I sensed that you didn't understand and that you might have thought I was rejecting you.

But I need to impress upon you that the "doors" I referred to in my last letter have been blown wide open *so quickly* that I'm still trying to catch up with all that's happened. I first met with Mary Ann on February 21st. In less than two months, you and I were talking on the telephone.

In less than two months!

And it's only been *eight months* since I made the initial *decision* to want to find you.

When Mary Ann told me she had some leads to find you, I thought she would be tracking you for months. I thought I'd be able to sit back and wait, maybe even relax for a while. After all, most searches take years!

But Mary Ann found you in less than a month!

Too, I haven't had a break from thinking about my adoption, whether to search for you, or what I'd do if/when I found you since last August.

I wasn't prepared for so many things to happen in such a short time: the decision to search, telling my adoptive father and Sonja about my desire to find you, receiving the nonidentifying information, giving the green light on the search itself, the discovery of you, your desire to contact me, my acceptance into your/my family, and your telling me that you loved me.

All this has been too much, too soon for me.

I wish I could have made you understand this today without hurting you.

April 19, 1985

Dear Ruth:

Isn't there a movie title, *Stop the World, I Want to Get Off?*

I want to slow things down a bit. I want to stop my adoption "world" from spinning in my mind for a little while. I want to stop processing thoughts and feelings about my adoption and to clear my mind.

I'm going to get away for a while. Maybe I'll go to the Cape. I think spending time near the ocean is what I need to help give me a different perspective on my adoption and to help me feel more comfortable with everything that's happened since August 1984.

May 3, 1985

Dear Ruth:

I have three days left in Provincetown before I return home.

When I first started this vacation, I thought about how I should be clear with you, the next time we speak, about what I want and what I need from you. I told myself that I should also strive to be consistent with you; for example, I shouldn't make plans to see you and then cancel them.

But today, on a beautiful run I had out to Race Point, I realized that I'm not always going to be able to be clear or consistent with you, no matter how hard I try.

And that's got to be okay.

Ours is a highly emotional relationship, one that has a built-in closeness because of our mother–daughter connection and our blood bond, but also has a limited emotional "comfort zone" to handle such closeness because we've never connected as mother and daughter. In reality, we're strangers. We have no established basis of trust. We don't even know yet whether we like each other.

While you're showing me that you feel okay keeping yourself (your "door"), your/my family, and your love wide open to me, I don't feel equally at ease.

So, for me, I think it has to be okay if, in the course of building a relationship with you, I sometimes seem to want to be close to you and then sometimes seem to be running away from you.

I think it's okay if both of us can open doors to each other as well as close them.

May 12, 1985

Dear Ruth:

I opened a door to you today. It felt okay at first, then a little uncomfortable.

I called you this morning to ask if we could try to get together again. You said yes, and we agreed to meet at your house on May 20th.

I asked if you would mind if I brought a friend with me. "For moral support," I explained. "I'd like someone to be there with me, if that's okay." (What I didn't tell you is that I need someone *familiar* to be with me. Knowing that I'm going to your "territory," where you'll be surrounded by things that make you feel secure, is unsettling to me. I need to have a friend along who can make me feel safe and secure.)

"That's fine, Amy," you agreed. "Ben, my husband, will be here, too. He doesn't go to work until late afternoon. Is that okay with you?"

"Sure," I said, as my mind whirred with a label to identify Ben's role in my life. Stepfather?, I wondered, then abandoned the thought as you spoke.

"I don't think my daughter Lorraine can make it, though," you told me.

"That's . . . uh . . . fine," I said, then breathed deeply. "You see, Ruth, to tell you the truth, it's okay if Lorraine can't be there. That makes me feel much better. I don't know if I'm ready to meet other members of the family. I think I'd like to see how things go between the two of us first before I start to get to know others."

"Well, they all really want to meet you, Amy," you quickly responded.

"I know," I answered, then wondered if I had detected a tone of disapproval in your voice.

"We can arrange another time," you said. "I'll have you here again for a cookout, and then you can meet Lorraine."

"Fine. But let's talk about that later, okay?" I asked, feeling a bit perturbed at the continued pursuit of my meeting Lorraine.

"Fine."

We then agreed upon a time for me to be at your house, and I double-checked the directions with you.

"Okay, I'll see you then," you said. "I love you, Amy."

The silence on the line was deafening in my ear.

"I . . . uh . . . loveyoutoo," I answered quickly, then hung up the phone.

May 14, 1985

Dear Ruth:

I wish I could communicate two things to you and have you understand and respect them.

First, I wish you didn't expect me to join your family group now or in the near future. I wish I didn't feel as if you were pushing this upon me and/or requiring it of our interactions with one another. I know that you love Lorraine and care for her. I know that part of the reason you want Lorraine and I to meet is so that *she* won't feel threatened by me or the fact that you're our mother.

My request is not intended to pass judgment on who Lorraine is as a person. I'm sure that she's very nice. And it doesn't matter to me whether you have other children, although it may matter more to them that I've made contact with you. But my search hasn't been and isn't for them.

Over time, I may feel comfortable meeting Lorraine and/or other members of your family. But right now, I only want to meet you.

Second, I wish I didn't feel as if you expect me to tell you that I love you. In our last conversation, I felt you wanted me to respond to you in kind.

But I don't know if I love you. In all honesty, I don't know if I even like you. How can I? I don't know you. Liking you and loving you are feelings that, for me, need to grow over time.

Perhaps it doesn't matter to you whether I tell you that I love you when you say it to me. Perhaps you're not waiting for me to say those three words to you. Perhaps my discomfort with this issue comes from me, from my telling you that I loved you not because I really do, but because I felt guilty about not saying it back.

I feel that our emotional connection with each other, whatever that will be, will make itself known over time. For now, it's hard to hear you say you love me. I don't trust it (I feel we haven't had a history that establishes it), I don't believe it (you don't know who I am, so how can you love someone you don't know?), and I'm unable to respond to it (it doesn't feel reciprocal on my part).

I wish you could be patient with me and let me get to know you in my own time. Perhaps then I can grow to love you and your/my family in the way you'd like me to—but at my own pace.

May 15, 1985

Dear Ruth:

I spent a lot of time today debating whether I should bring you something when I visit you in a few days. I couldn't decide what I would bring you: a small gift, a bunch of flowers, or a home-baked good.

I pored through all my recipe books until I finally slammed the last one shut and cried out, "Of course! I know *exactly* what I'll bring her!"

I rummaged through a stack of photo albums, finally located my baby pictures, pulled out two of the cutest (at least in my opinion!) portraits, and placed them in an envelope for you.

May 20, 1985

Dear Ruth:

I've been dressed and ready to go since nine o'clock this morning. My friend isn't picking me up until noon!

I'm thinking of you right now and wondering what you're doing, wondering what you're thinking.

Are you as nervous as I am? (My hand is shaking as I write this.)

Are you rehearsing what you'll say to me? (I don't know what to call you: Ruth, Mom, or Mrs. Roberts. I don't know how to start our conversation: "Say, how about those Red Sox?," or "Nice weather we've been having, isn't it?," or "So, what have you been doing for the last thirty-one years?")

Are you restless and edgy? (I've been pacing back and forth for several minutes.)

Are you scared? *(I'm petrified!)*

Dear Ruth:

When my friend and I pulled into your driveway at one o'clock this afternoon (we were right on time—was that okay, or did that make me appear too anxious?), I simply breathed a deep sigh, then said aloud, "This is it."

I don't remember getting out of the car or walking up the brick path to your front door. But I do remember how fast my heart was beating. I thought it would pound right out of my chest.

Before I could even knock on the screen door, you appeared and opened the door to let us in.

One voice in my head cried out to me: "This is your birthmother! Can you believe it? She's standing right there in front of you!" But another voice cautioned: "You're in the house of a perfect stranger. You know nothing about this person. Be careful! Keep your distance." The conflicting voices made me feel even more nervous than I already was.

So I didn't know what to do when I first saw you. Should I have hugged you? Should I have shaken your hand?

Or should I have done exactly as I did: completely forget about introducing my friend to you (I heard you exchange introductions with each other as I muttered to myself, "Nice going, Amy"), walk into your kitchen, look at the cluttered counters and dishes piled in the sink, and say without thinking, "What a *beautiful* kitchen!"

I could have died from embarrassment.

You seemed so relaxed and under control. You suggested that we sit outside, around a table on the porch, because it was such a gorgeous spring day. You handed me a plate of pastries to take outside and asked my friend to carry coffee cups as you steered us out the door to the porch.

We sat down at the table. You served us coffee.

Ben came out of the house then and introduced himself. I shook his hand.

"Say," he said to my friend, "can I show you the garden out back?"

I watched as my safety and security said "Sure," got up from the seat next to me, and walked away.

I didn't know what to do.

I didn't know what to say.

So I busied myself with cream and sugar for my coffee.

Then, as I started to pull off my jacket, I felt the envelope in my pocket. "I brought you these," I blurted out as I handed you the envelope.

When you opened the envelope and saw the pictures, you smiled and stared at them for several moments.

"Thank you, Amy," you finally said. "May I make copies of these and return them to you?"

"They're yours to keep," I replied.

"How thoughtful," you commented, then excused yourself, went into the house, and returned with a stack of pictures.

"I guess we were both thinking along the same lines. I went through my pictures last night and selected some I thought you'd like to look at." The first one you handed to me was a black-and-white photograph of a teenage girl in a plaid dress.

"That's me," you said. "I was pregnant with you at the time, but not showing." My eyes automatically looked at your stomach in the photo. I thought to myself, "There I am."

"You can keep that one, Amy. But that's the only one I have of me at that time. The rest of these pictures are of your family."

I thought to myself, "Oh, great," but smiled.

"Let me start with your brother and sisters," you said as you moved your chair closer to mine.

For the next several minutes, you showed me pictures of your children, you and your husband, and an assortment of indistinguishable people who were identified by your lengthy explanations that were, I think, supposed to make me feel as though I was part of the family. But I didn't care about any of the people you described to me.

Instead, I cast frequent and furtive glances at the photo of you while you were pregnant with me that was lying on the table. *That* picture meant a great deal more to me than any number of pictures of your/my family.

That picture was about you and me.

You finished describing the stack of photos by showing me a picture of you holding a baby in your arms and smiling at the camera. I looked at the teenage picture of you, then at you holding the baby. Suddenly, I wanted to cry.

"Are there any pictures that you'd like copies of?" you asked me.

I blinked hard as my eyes filled with tears.

"Amy?"

"Just once," I said softly, looking down at the table to

avoid your eyes, "I'd like to see a picture of me as a baby, with a mother holding me. My dad doesn't have any pictures from his marriage with my adoptive mother—I think she took them all with her when they were divorced— so I don't have pictures of Margery holding me. There are no pictures of my foster mother holding me. And when my stepmother came into my life, I was seven—beyond the size of being held and beyond being a baby.

"It makes me sad to see you holding your daughter in your arms in that picture."

"That's my son," you commented as you looked at the picture.

"Okay, your son," I corrected myself, with a trace of impatience in my voice. "I can't tell. They all look alike at that age. But what's important is that you're *holding* him. You're his mother and you're *holding* him."

You arose from your chair and stood next to me.

"Amy, I'm your mother and I can hold you now." You then leaned over, wrapped your arms around my shoulders, and pulled me tightly to you.

Your hold startled me at first. Then I realized that you were trying to help me through my pain—that you were my *mother* and *you were holding me.*

"You know, Amy," you said as you rubbed my shoulders, then let me go and sat down next to me, "after I delivered the oldest of your siblings, my son, I cried. I held on to him very tightly. I didn't want to let him go. I was afraid that he would be taken away from me, too."

I wiped the tears from my eyes. "That must have been painful for you."

"It was. I've never forgotten you. I've never stopped thinking about you and I've never stopped caring. Every October third, I remember it's your birthday and I wonder what you're doing and how you're doing."

I smiled. "For so long, I've wondered about you, too—who you were and why you gave me away."

"We lost each other, Amy, many years ago. Now we've found each other. Finding you has made me feel complete again. It's made me whole."

I nodded. "Finding you is giving me the answers I need so I can feel whole. I've always thought of myself as an incomplete puzzle that I'd never be able to put together. But you're helping me to find out so many things. I want to hear more."

"Like what?"

"Well, I've always wondered what time I was born and where I was born."

"You were born in St. Joseph's Hospital, which is only about thirty minutes from here, in the same town where I was staying with my aunt and uncle. You were born between three and four in the morning."

I let this information sink in.

"Was it a difficult birth?"

You shook your head. "No. There were no complications. You were pretty easy."

"Did my father know about me?"

Your eyebrows furrowed and your face instantly lost its tenderness. "No, Amy. I didn't tell him. I didn't care to tell him. I just wanted him out of my life."

"What was my father's name?"

Your entire body tensed. "Why do you need to know that?" you asked a bit sharply.

I shrugged my shoulders. "Because I'm interested. Because he was my father. Because—"

"I don't want to talk about him," you interrupted. "He wasn't a very nice man. He was . . . he was quite abusive. I don't think he's someone you want to know."

"I don't want to *know* him, Ruth. I'd just like to know what his name was, what his family history was, his medical history—you know, the same information I need from you."

"I don't remember his name," you said. "But I do know that he was healthy."

"What about his family? Was there any—"

You cut me off. "Later, Amy, if you want, I'll try to find out these things. But right now, please be satisfied with the information I've given to you. Your father is a very painful subject for me. I don't want him in my life anymore."

Before I could respond, Ben and my friend returned then from their garden walk. You seemed quite relieved to see them. I let the subject of my birthfather drop.

Ben offered to take our pictures. He retrieved an instamatic camera from the house and patiently posed first me, then you, then the two of us.

As we returned to the porch to sit down, I suddenly realized how tired I felt. My body was weary, as if I had just run seven miles in the heat. My mind felt drained, as if there was nothing more it could handle at the moment.

The idea of going home, relaxing in a hot bath, and then taking a long nap seemed very appealing.

I looked at you and noticed that you seemed weary, too.

So, after some small talk, I told you I must be going. You said that you'd call me soon.

As we stood up to leave, you opened your arms to me and pulled me close to you.

Tentatively, I placed my arms around your shoulders. I realized, at that moment, as I felt your arms around me and mine around you, that I had achieved what I had once felt would be the hardest thing I could ever do in my life:

I had found my beginnings.

I had found my answers.

I had found you, my birthmother.

May 23, 1985

Dear Ruth:

Today I received a "feelings-style" greeting card from you, titled "It's Okay." The verse begins, "It's okay to be afraid of things we don't understand. . . ."

Inside the card, you wrote how nice it was to see me and thanked me for the baby pictures.

"I shall treasure them always," you wrote.

You said that I've healed a scar in your life that only I could heal. It was nice to know that where you once felt pain (the scar), you could now feel a sense of healing.

And I, too, have felt a certain sense of peace from our

visit. You've given me the answers that I've wanted and needed, the answers that only you could give me.

As I closed the card I realized that if I never saw you again, that would be okay.

I'm satisfied with what you've given me already. I don't need to ask you to give me more.

May 25, 1985

Dear Ruth:

On my desk, in front of me, are the three pictures Ben took of us at your house.

There's one of you alone. You're smiling at the camera. The sun is in your eyes, making you squint. You're wearing pink pants and a white sweater. The day is warm, so your sleeves are rolled up above your elbows.

When my friend looked at the pictures on the way home, she said that our faces looked alike. "You both have similar cheeks when you smile," she pointed out. At a stop light, I looked at the pictures. But I couldn't see any similarity between us.

I look now at the pictures of you and me together. I glance back and forth, from me to you and you to me, but I can't discern any resemblance. This disappoints me. I think I had expectations, prior to seeing you, that we would look just like each other, or at least share some visible similarities.

But no, I can't see anything in common at all.

June 2, 1985

Dear Ruth:

You called me today to invite my friend and me to a cookout at your house the following Saturday.

"Lorraine is coming, and she really wants to meet you," you told me.

I looked at my calendar. I had no scheduled plans. I really didn't want to go but it was apparent, from your expectant tone of voice, that you wanted me to.

I thought to myself, "What would be the big deal, visiting Ruth again and meeting Lorraine? If it means a lot to Ruth, maybe I should do it."

So I told you that I was free.

June 15, 1985

Dear Ruth:

The cookout was yesterday. The weather was great and the food was delicious. Seeing you again felt fine, but meeting Lorraine was a little awkward.

My friend and I had no sooner arrived, and Lorraine and I had just been introduced to each other, when you said, "I don't believe it! I don't have any hot dogs. Lorraine, why don't you drive to the store with Amy to pick up a couple of packages."

Before I could consider whether the lack of hot dogs was a contrived plan to get Lorraine and me together (after all, who *doesn't* have the hot dogs for a cookout?), we were in the car driving to the grocery store.

I didn't know what to say to her. But she seemed relaxed and began talking to me about her boyfriend.

I remember thinking to myself, "Is this 'sister talk'?" So I tried to offer her appropriately mature conversation and advice.

When we returned to your home, the day went by quickly and smoothly. You had a chance to learn more about me in my present life, as we talked of things other than the adoption because of Lorraine's presence.

In retrospect, I realize that having Lorraine there provided us both with an opportunity to interact with one another without focusing on the common basis of the adoption. I even forgot, for most of the afternoon, that you were my birthmother. Instead, the get-together felt like a social invitation from a neighbor, where the conversation is light and the mood is easygoing.

The only time I was reminded of the connection for the get-together was when Ben once again brought out the instamatic and took pictures—this time of Lorraine and me, then you, me, and Lorraine. (I have them propped on the desk in front of me, along with the others.)

July 21, 1985

Dear Ruth:

Writing my first book has kept me busy lately, but I was finally able to have you and Ben to my house for lunch last weekend.

This was the first time I've seen you without my friend with me. While it still felt a bit awkward—because I really don't know you very well and because what I needed to learn from you about my adoption has already been discussed—I think that the time we spent together was pleasant.

I wish, though, that your conversation focused less on family members. I wish that you'd stop identifying members of your family as *my* sisters, *my* aunts, etc. That makes me feel like I'm being pulled into your family before I'm ready.

I just don't think of *your* family as *my* family.

I don't know if I ever will.

August 19, 1985

Dear Ruth:

My parents came down last weekend. I told them that I had met with you, and I related all the information you told me about my adoption. I showed them your teenage picture and all the pictures Ben took of us.

As we were eating dinner, I realized that less than one month ago, you and Ben had been sitting across from me at the table, where my dad and Sonja were now sitting.

I realized, too, that I was more relaxed, more talkative, and much happier in the company of my dad and Sonja. They felt so safe and secure to me.

As they were getting ready to leave, I found that I didn't want them to go. I felt a wall of loneliness closing in around me that I've never felt before when I've parted from them.

So I said something to them that surprised even me, because I've never said anything like it before:

"Do you mind if we spend more time together—all of us? I feel like we don't get to see each other a whole lot. I think sometimes I miss being with you. We could go out to dinner or maybe see a movie, or . . ."

I had started to cry, but had shed only a few tears before I started laughing.

"Isn't this silly? I can't make up my mind how I feel! I'm sad and happy at the same time. I think searching for Ruth has brought my past to a close, that makes me a little sad because it's all I've thought about for so long. But finding her has made me realize that I'm happy to be where I am, with you as my parents. Despite all of our problems, I think I came out of my childhood okay. I think *we're* okay.

"Finding Ruth has made me more appreciative of what I have, not what I have not."

Then I hugged my dad and told him that I loved him.

I turned to face Sonja.

Sonja and I have rarely been physical or emotionally expressive with each other.

But I threw my arms around her and whispered in her ear, "I love you, Mom."

I don't know what my parents thought of my tears or my sudden need to be with them but, for that moment, nothing I've ever done or said before has made more sense to me than hugging my parents and telling them that I loved them.

September 9, 1985

Dear Ruth:

I've been thinking lately about the discomfort I originally felt at the end of our first telephone conversation (when I heard about the members of your/my family and learned that you, and others, wanted to welcome me as a member of your/my family) and about my last emotional interaction with my parents.

Last night, I reread all the letters I've written to you since August 1984 and came to a powerful understanding of why I felt the way I did about you and about my parents.

I haven't yet claimed a family as my own.

In my struggle as an adopted person to feel like I belong somewhere, I've never felt that I belonged to a family, even my adoptive family. For example, I've never once proclaimed,

"I'm a Dean," even though I love my father, Sonja, and Margery.

And although I love the relatives on my father's side and I spend all the major holidays—Easter, Thanksgiving, and Christmas—with relatives on Sonja's side, I've never once believed that I belonged to either or both groups of people.

Of all the families I've had—and still have—in my life, there's not one to which I've felt I truly belonged.

Sonja's family is Scandinavian. They all have blond hair and blue eyes and are fair-skinned. My grandmother spoke with a Swedish accent, calling jam "yam" and jelly "yelly." I always knew when Sonja was talking on the phone with her; the conversation was in Swedish, except for the occasional mention of my name or my father's name.

My grandmother was an excellent cook whose specialty was baked goods: cookies, breads, and pastries. When she died, her recipes died along with her. My father once remarked that I should have spent a few afternoons with her before she died, learning how to make her Swedish treats.

I didn't feel that it was my place to do that.

My father's family has black hair and blue or hazel eyes. My dad grew up in a large family where the children played together very competitively. The drive to win and succeed has stayed with them throughout their adult lives. Today, I know the source of my own ambition and competitive edge.

But the members of the Dean family are scattered across the country. We haven't been together, as a family, in over twenty years.

Margery's family is my family, too. But I have no idea where they are or how to locate them.

Your family is unknown to me, yet related by one of the bonds considered by many to be the strongest—blood.

I haven't yet claimed a family, but I realize now that I can claim, as mine, *any* or *all* families I want to, whether these families are related to me through biological ties, adoption, foster parenting, or even the connection of friendship.
   You might think that I would revel in this realization, knowing that I have a choice, because of the sense of powerlessness I've felt for most of my life.
   But, to me, claiming a family is scary.

Sometimes I think I've spent most of my life opening and closing doors to people who are part of my adoptive family. Over the years, I've felt my aunts and uncles, my cousins, and my grandmother try to get close to me through their words and their actions, but I've kept everyone at arm's length, both physically and emotionally (everyone, that is, except for my dad).
   I guess I've always believed that if I let these people into my life—if I have fun with them, derive comfort from their company, grow closer to them, and feel love for

them—then they're going to go away from me and I'll lose all those wonderful things.

I fear the love they've shown or want to show me not because of the strength of that feeling, but because of the threat of how it will feel if/when I lose that feeling. So, rather than open a door to any family member, I've kept it firmly shut.

In declining to claim a family up to this point in my life, I've held on to the belief that I need to protect myself from the greatest consequence of my adoption: *loss*.

I haven't wanted to claim a family because I don't want to lose a family. I don't want to stake an emotional interest in something that might not last.

That's because I've always believed: *Families aren't forever.*

Let me give you examples of why I have such a belief.

Mom Fowler told me once about a time when she heard Margery, my dad, and me on the porch of her house. My parents and I had just spent the weekend together, and I was being returned to the Fowlers' care.

As Mom Fowler looked out the window, she heard my father call out, "Family group! Family group!" and saw the three of us—mother, father, and child—form a small football-style huddle, our arms around each other.

That was the family group I began with. That was the family group that wanted me. That was the family group that encircled me with love. That was the family group where I felt I belonged. And that was the family group that I lost.

Families don't last forever.

And then there was Mom and Dad Fowler's home, filled

with love, warmth, and two older foster brothers. Even after my dad married Sonja, I talked about wanting to go back to live with the Fowlers.

Families don't last forever:

The difficulties that Sonja and I had in harmonizing as mother and daughter not only pulled her and me apart but also prevented my father from being close to both of us at the same time.

Families don't last forever.

And now you expect me to feel safe and secure in your/my family. You want me to meet the members of your family and to spend holidays with you (you brought up your/my family's plans for this coming Thanksgiving and Christmas when you and Ben came to my house for lunch).

To me, families are scary. Families can hurt. Families can disappoint. Families can fall apart.

Families don't last forever.

But finding you has given me a whole new outlook on families. I'm ready now to claim a family.

I *am a Dean.* Bruce Dean is my father, Margery Dean was my adoptive mother, and Sonja Dean has been my mother for most of my life. *I am a Dean.*

Since you're my birthmother, you certainly have a place in my life. But I don't see your/my family as having a place in my life.

I want and need my feelings of family safety and security to come from Bruce and Sonja Dean—my mother and father—and from the members of each of their families.

October 3, 1985

Dear Ruth:

Today I received a birthday card from you, Mom and Dad Fowler, and my parents. (If Margery were alive, I think I would have received one from her, too!)

Seeing your name and the others on the cards reminded me of how I have always purchased two Mother's day cards: one for Sonja and one for Mom Fowler. (And, if Margery were alive, I'd buy one for her, too!).

Now you'll be added to my Mother's Day card list!

November 29, 1985

Dear Ruth:

This past Thanksgiving holiday was one of the nicest ones I've ever had with my parents and Sonja's family. I've known them (and they've known me) since I was seven years old; that's the longest I've ever been with one family. I realized how nice it felt to have that sense of consistency.

I even helped Sonja in the kitchen, and we didn't argue once!

As I was leaving, one of my aunts remarked, "Amy, I don't know what it is about you today, but you look great. You're positively glowing. You seem so happy. You seem so *together*."

As I drove home, I realized that finding you and learning about the circumstances of my adoption have enabled me to feel that way.

I *do* feel together.

I feel at peace with myself, at one with myself.

Finding you, and finding answers, has done that for me.

December 23, 1985

Dear Ruth:

I'm sitting here at my desk, feeling rather stunned and shaken. I've just finished reading a letter you wrote after I visited you on December 20th, when I came down to exchange Christmas presents. From the sound of your letter, you have some strong feelings—mostly anger directed at me—about the way I acted (in your eyes) during this visit.

While I feel bad that I've apparently hurt you and made you unhappy, I don't understand your anger. It seems to be directed at what I'm capable of giving to you—and receiving from you—at this point in our interactions with each other.

You mentioned how hurt you were that I didn't hug you when I came into your house. Ruth, I'm just getting used to hugging Sonja when I see her, and she's been my mother for twenty-four years! I've never been much of a hugger, except with my dad. That kind of physical closeness is difficult for me.

I've known you (or, I should say, I've hardly known you)

for less than *seven months*. While you may feel comfortable hugging me, *I don't*.

I wish you didn't interpret my not hugging you as a reflection of how I may or may not feel about you. To me a hug is an action that makes me quite uncomfortable. I wish that you could accept this and let me give you a hug when I'm ready, in my own time.

I wish that you could also place less emphasis on a hug's symbolic gesture of affection and look at the fact that I cared enough to want to see you and to celebrate, in a small way, an important family holiday.

In your letter, you also commented that you had spent hours cleaning the house and making sure everything was just right for me. You were then distressed when I didn't even take off my coat. To you, that action made it seem as if I was negating the effort that you had put in to make sure that I'd be comfortable in your home.

Ruth, I didn't want to make my visit a big deal. I told you that I was just dropping by. I told you I couldn't stay long before I even arrived. What difference did it make whether my coat was on or off? *I was there!*

You mentioned also that my actions made it seem as if I was a stranger in your house. *But I am a stranger.* You may not view me as one, but that's how I feel!

I wish you could understand how pressured you make me feel at times, which makes it uncomfortable for me to be around you.

I'm sorry I made you so upset that you had to write me

such an angry letter. But I don't know how to give you what you want when what you want isn't what *I* want.

December 26, 1985

Dear Ruth:

You've called a few times to invite me to get together with your family. I've declined. I'm just not comfortable with your family. I don't feel that's where I belong.

January 5, 1986

Dear Ruth:

The bustle of the holiday season has given me a chance to gain a little perspective on the letter you wrote me. Maybe what I have to say in this letter will help you understand me better so you can give me a little more leeway in our future interactions.

Do you remember, in an earlier letter, when I asked you which was stronger: an emotional bond or a blood bond? I think it might help you to understand me a little better if you keep in mind that you have a blood bond with a family that raised you. You have children who have a blood bond with you, who you raised. And you have me, your first child and another blood bond.

But you're the first blood bond I've had in my life. To me, such a connection is foreign. It doesn't happen automatically, just because you're my biological mother. Emotional bonds are what I've known and developed in my life. They haven't happened automatically. My dad, my foster parents, and Sonja and I have had to *work* on developing trust and consistency, support and security, and caring and love.

Because the emotional bond is more familiar, I require more time to develop such a bond.

I *can't* show you instant warmth and affection. I *can't* be as open with you as you are with me.

I need more room to let this emotional closeness grow.

If you expect me to say or do things in ways that are comfortable or familiar to you, then I'll always feel pressure when being with you. And I don't think that's right.

I think it's important that we both be comfortable with one another. If we're not, then we're only going to continue to have difficulties and disappointments.

February 18, 1986

Dear Ruth:

Sometimes I feel that I've failed as an adoptee who searched.

The stories of adoptee–birthmother reunions that I read about in magazines and newspapers and the ones that I see on talk shows have happy endings where the adoptee and the birthmother become close friends—even best friends. These people never seem to have any difficulties bonding emotionally or physically with one another. They often proclaim, "From the moment I laid eyes on her/him, I knew it was like a fairy tale come true. We're friends for life." Some adoptees' stories even relate that the birthparents meet the adoptive parents, and then everyone gets along really well—like one, big happy family.

Why wasn't our reunion like a dream come true?

Sometimes I feel that I've done something wrong to make it turn out the way it has.

March 4, 1986

Dear Ruth:

One of my long-distance friends (who isn't adopted) wrote to me today, replying to a letter I recently sent her in which I detailed everything that has happened between you and me.

She wrote: "Amy, don't be upset with yourself. I think your reunion story is more typical than you may realize. We only hear the great stories of mother and child reuniting in the depths of love. Your reaction and your birthmother's reaction are probably more common than we're led to believe. I don't think it will be an easy path for either of you. But I think that's to be expected."

I think about how true my friend's words are. She's right; we don't hear of the painful or distressing reunions, for who would want to know about them? No magazine editor or talk show host would want to recount a story such as ours, which ends, on both parts, with disappointment, unmet expectations, and no clear resolution.

When we first saw each other, Ruth, we didn't fall into each other's arms. We haven't become bosom buddies. We're still struggling, first together, and now apart, to find a happy medium, a balance of give and take that makes us both happy.

We haven't yet achieved a relationship that gives each of us what we need or want.

But I think that we should be able to look at where we're at right now and say, "It's okay."

Sure, some reunions turn out to be all "sugar and spice." But some are "oil and water." Some are like a roller coaster ride. And some are as difficult to swallow as unsweetened lemon juice.

Reunion outcomes should be allowed to be as unique, varied, and fluctuating as the individuals involved in them.

March 25, 1986

Dear Ruth:

I want you to know one thing: *My search for you has been very satisfying to me, despite our differences.*

I now have answers to the mysteries of my life: where I came from, who you are, and why I was placed for adoption.

You have helped me to bring my past to rest.

While I don't know what the next step for us will be, I'm willing to stick it out. Even though I can't give you what you want or need (you seem to want and expect more from me than I can give), you've given me what I've wanted and needed. For now, I don't expect more.

I guess that means that we're at an impasse.

But it could also mean that we're just taking some time before we reach out to a different level with each other.

Who knows what lies ahead for us?

Only time will tell what the next step for us will be.

Epilogue

Don't you think that everyone looks back on their child-hood with a certain amount of bitterness and regret about something? It doesn't have to ruin your life.... Aren't you tired of it all? Bore, bore, bore!
—ERNEST THOMPSON
On Golden Pond

I don't think my birthmother will ever be my mother. I have a nice relationship with her, but I have said many times that I'm glad I was adopted. My adopted mother was my mother no matter what.
—SUZANNE BEEBE
co-founder of TRY (Today Unites Yesterday),
a Northampton (Massachusetts)-based, nonprofit resource
and support organization for birthparents
and adoptees wishing to pursue searches.

From late 1986 to 1989, the only contact I had with my birthmother was through occasional holiday cards. Sometimes we included a brief note in the cards—"Real busy, but thinking of you"—but often there was only a signature.

In the fall of 1989, I started to work on issues related to my adoption with a therapist. We explored how my sense of loss and powerlessness had affected, and sometimes still affects, many areas of my life. Since writing has always helped me to shed light on some of my unrealized thoughts and feelings, I began writing this book.

During that time, I contacted my birthmother to reopen

a door to her, to let her know that I was willing to explore a renewed relationship with her. She informed me that she was going through a painful and abusive divorce and felt that it was best that she place her emotional energy in getting through it. But she said that she was happy I had contacted her, still thought of me, and loved me.

In March 1990, I contacted the hospital where I was born to find out how I could obtain information in my birth records about my birthfather. They informed me that I could go to probate court to have my birthmother authorize opening the records.

My birthmother vehemently refused my request to open my birth records for this information. She told me that I had no right to open *her* records and that I should "be satisfied" with the information she had already given me about my birthfather.

Even though I tried to impress upon her that the birth records were my records, too; that my medical information was still incomplete without my birthfather's background; and that I *did* have a right to know because, no matter what her relationship with my birthfather had been, *he* was my biological father, she wouldn't budge.

March 19, 1990, was the last time I spoke with my birthmother.

In an earlier letter to my birthmother, I had written:
"I think it's okay if both of us can open doors to each other as well as close them."

It seems now as if both doors are closed.

When, or if, they will open again remains to be seen.

Afterword: The Adoptee's Desire to Search

MARY ANN ULEVICH, ACSW, LICSW
Director of Social Services
Worcester Children's Friend Society
Worcester, Massachusetts

... as the baby boom generation ages, more and more of them are interested in information about and contact with biological family members. A survey done in 1984 estimated that 500,000 adult adoptees were either in the process of seeking their birth parents or had successfully located them. A Harvard University study recently estimated that 96 percent of all birthmothers contemplate a search, and more than 60 percent undertake one.
—EILEEN KUPERSCHMID,
"A Search for Roots," *The Boston Globe*, April 30, 1990

Child welfare agencies that have traditionally offered adoption services to parents and birthparents have expanded these services to include adoptees. Typically, adoption agencies worked with birthparents and adoptive parents through the completion of legalized adoption. Services beyond this goal were usually at the request of adoptive parents. Requests ranged from additional medical information if a child was suspected of having an inherited disease or disability to assistance in explaining adoption to a child to extreme situations in which adoptive parents asked for the removal of a child if serious problems were not resolved. In some cases, adoptive parents sought assistance during the adolescence of their adopted children—a period of development that is frequently marked by adjustment problems for adolescents in general. The tension between parents and their children at this time may be exacerbated by the complexities of adoption. Probably many more parents sought assistance from mental health professionals, choosing not to return to the adoption agency lest they be seen as inadequate parents.

Adoptees' requests for services from the agency that handled their adoption are a fairly recent phenomenon. Through the years, confidentiality has been promised both to birthparents and to adoptive parents. The law supports confidentiality. However, the desire of adoptees to have information about their biological origins is recognized as normal and natural. Adoptees, through no decision of their own, have been barred access to that information. The decision to search—to seek information ranging from nonidentifying physical descriptions and medical information to a reunion with birth parents—is accepted as a reasonable request.

The request to search is presented in a unique manner by each adoptee. There are, however, common themes that I and my colleagues have noted. The first theme centers on the role of the adoptive parents. Discussion with adoptive parents usually precedes the first telephone call; sometimes this is the first time an adoptee learns the name of the adoption agency. On more than one occasion, adoptive parents have telephoned to pave the way for their adult adopted child. In other instances, adoptive parents are deceased and an adoptee describes a "freedom" to request a search, fearing that such a request while adoptive parents were alive might have been misunderstood, perhaps even considered a rejection or criticism of their parenting.

Of note, however, is the theme of the adoptive parents' permission to learn about one's biological roots. Whether this permission is sought and received, sought and withheld, or not sought at all is discussed by the social worker and the adoptee. However, the quality of the relationship between adoptees and adoptive parents is not used solely as a determinant for proceeding with the search. The request to search is generally understood as a natural development.

The second theme centers on the timing of the request. Requests frequently are made after many years of thinking about doing so. What, then, prompts the request? Sometimes a change in one's life such as college graduation, marriage, divorce, the birth of a child, illness, or the death of an adoptive parent prompts an adoptee to telephone. But such an event sometimes merely fuels the desire and is not enough to bolster the courage necessary to make the call. A television show, a newspaper article, or a friend's encouragement may provide the final nudge. Once a request is made, however, time takes on an interesting dimension for many adoptees. A sense of urgency has been noted with some people. There may be fear that if contact is not made immediately, a birthparent may no longer be available, may not even be alive if another day goes by without contact. It is as if all the thinking and agonizing over the desire to search have been collapsed into a driven, immediate need. For other adoptees, the process moves almost too quickly, as if yet more time is needed to prepare for the outcome—an outcome that may be both dreaded and longed for. Once again, during the search process, the social worker and the adoptee discuss expectations, fears, and wishes. The pressure of time may be allayed or heightened. The clock ticks on tolerably or impatiently.

The third theme centers on the content of the request. There is an assumption that there are compelling reasons to find out about oneself. Emotions spark the request; it is not simply an intellectual pursuit. The "wish to know," to "make a connection," to "have an understanding," and to "gaze upon my mother's face" are all valid requests. Many adoptees decide to seek information on two levels. The first is to ask for nonidentifying information. This includes a medical history, including psychiatric disorders and alcoholism, and reasons why the adoptee was released for adoption. Sometimes physical descriptions, personality characteristics, talents, and interests are sought. Some adoptees hope to hear that their fantasies about birthparents are fact. Nonidentifying information satisfies some adoptees, and they do not request contact with birthparents. Some are satisfied for a time and then request that we seek a reunion for them with birthparents. This leads to the fourth theme.

The second level is the request for identifying information, for a meeting and/or contact with a birthparent, and it is presented in a number of ways. A common theme, however, is a wish to meet a birthparent, typically a birthmother, "if she wants to meet me." Even when adoptees assert a desire to meet a birthparent, I and my colleagues have noted a protective stance by adoptees. This stance may be marked by a wish not to "disrupt" birthparents and a protestation that they will understand if birthparents decline permission to release identifying information necessary for a reunion. But who does this stance protect? Adoptees may wish not to be rejected again by a birthparent or may anticipate that rejection will be the only response to their request. The social worker and the adoptee discuss this theme in an attempt to locate the request where it began—with the adoptee. Confronting all that the request and the ensuing events that it precipitates is a crucial part of the search process. This helps to prepare the adoptee for the outcome.

The fifth theme we have identified is that few, if any, adoptees develop a plan to be involved on an ongoing basis with a birthparent. It is too difficult to plan when there are so many unknowns. Adoptees worry about being a disappointment to their birthparents. Birthparents worry that the adoptee will be angry, hurt, unforgiving, or disappointed with them. What about siblings? What about extended families? What about spouses who did not know about the child surrendered for adoption? What if the adoptee and the birthparent have different expectations? This has proved to be the case on several occasions. For some adoptees, one reunion may be enough. For some birthparents, the wish to re-create a birth family and to "make up" for the decision to release a child for adoption is overwhelming. The dimensions and complications are layered with emotion and opportunity for growth as well as for pain. The need for support for birthparents, adoptees, and adoptive parents is crucial.

In this discussion I have referred to adoptees and birthparents without regard to gender. However, the experience at our agency, mirrored in other adoption agencies, is that female adoptees requesting a search outnumber male adoptees. Further, the search typically centers on the birthmother. Following a reunion with a birthmother, adoptees may seek information about their birthfathers from their birthmothers. But the request for a search for a birthfather is unusual. We can speculate on these observations based upon cultural, emotional, and psychological dynamics. In this discussion, I merely note them.

In conclusion, the adoptee's desire to search for biological roots is accepted as natural and normal. When an adoptee requests assistance from an agency, the response should be "Of course you want to know" and not merely "Why do you want to know?" The process is a pursuit to "make a connection" and "to finally know," and we welcome opportunities to assist in that healthy pursuit.

Notice

Call for Papers

The author is interested in collecting the stories of adoptees and/or birthparents who have searched in order to compile a book that details the different experiences, outcomes, and reunions of adoptees and their birthparents.

If you would be interested in contributing your story, please contact Amy E. Dean, c/o Pharos Books—Adoption Stories, 200 Park Avenue, New York, NY 10166 for further details.